Sir Spencer Walpole

The Electorate and the Legislature

Sir Spencer Walpole
The Electorate and the Legislature
ISBN/EAN: 9783744729550
Printed in Europe, USA, Canada, Australia, Japan
Cover: Foto ©ninafisch / pixelio.de

More available books at **www.hansebooks.com**

THE
ELECTORATE
AND
THE LEGISLATURE

BY

SPENCER WALPOLE

AUTHOR OF "THE HISTORY OF ENGLAND FROM 1815"

London
MACMILLAN AND CO.
1881

The Right of Translation and Reproduction is Reserved

PREFACE

A WRITER who professes to describe "the electorate and legislature" of the United Kingdom is necessarily forced to travel over many chapters of the constitutional history of England. In doing so he has the advantage of clear guidance. The constitutional history of England to the reign of Henry VII. has been written by Mr. Stubbs; from the accession of Henry VII. to the death of George II. by Mr. Hallam; from the accession of George III. to the present time by Sir Erskine May. But the English Constitution has also been described by De Lolme and Lord Russell in former generations and by Mr. Freeman and Mr. Bagehot in our own time. The precedents of proceedings in the House of Commons were collected more than sixty years ago by Mr. Hatsall. The law and practice of Parliament has been described in recent years by Sir Erskine May.

Independent researches, made for a larger object, have also enabled the author of this book to add to some extent to the information which is thus accessible to the ordinary student. But he desires, on the first page of the work, to acknowledge the debt under which he lies to the authorities whom he has already named. The acknowledgment is the more necessary because in a little book of this character it is impossible to give the references which would be inserted in a larger work. To all the authorities he has named he is under an obligation; to three of them—Mr. Hallam, Mr. Stubbs, and Sir Erskine May, he is specially indebted. Sir Erskine May's work on Parliamentary Practice is the substructure on which every writer on Parliament must build. The great works of Mr. Hallam and Mr. Stubbs are too well known to require a compliment; but they are possibly susceptible to a criticism. Mr. Hallam's labours have perhaps done more than Mr. Stubbs's researches to give the general reader a clear idea of constitutional progress, but Mr. Stubbs's work has done more to assist the student than Mr. Hallam's history. Mr. Hallam excels in manner, Mr. Stubbs in matter: Mr. Hallam is superior to Mr. Stubbs in his generalisations; Mr. Stubbs to Mr. Hallam in the copiousness of his details.

LONDON, *June*, 1881.

CONTENTS

CHAPTER I.
PARLIAMENT 1

CHAPTER II.
THE HOUSE OF LORDS 25

CHAPTER III.
THE HOUSE OF COMMONS 47

CHAPTER IV.
PARLIAMENTARY QUALIFICATION AND ELECTORAL CORRUPTION 67

CHAPTER V.
PREROGATIVE AND PRIVILEGE 86

CHAPTER VI.

PUBLIC AND PRIVATE BILLS 107

CHAPTER VII.

SUPPLY 130

CHAPTER VIII.

ORDER AND OBSTRUCTION 143

THE
ELECTORATE AND THE LEGISLATURE.

CHAPTER I.

PARLIAMENT.

IN the second book of the *Iliad*, when Ulysses checks the flight of the Greeks, he addresses arguments to the leaders, he arrests the common people by blows. But, in the nineteenth century, when a modern statesman, gifted with the eloquence of Ulysses, desires to change the policy which a nation is pursuing, he addresses his arguments to the populace; he reserves his blows—blows of rhetoric—for their leaders. The difference between the conduct of Ulysses and that of the modern statesman is due of course to revolutions both in manners and government. Now, as in the olden time, men reason with those whom they wish to convert. It would have been a waste of time and breath if Ulysses had endeavoured to convince the masses; the modern statesman knows that it is useless to convert the people's leaders if the people themselves do not embrace their leaders' policy. In Homer the people die and suffer for the sins of Agamemnon, just as, in the Bible, the people die and suffer for the sins of David. The people in the nineteenth century, instead of dying for their leaders' sins, take the more sensible course of expelling them from power.

The change in the position of the people, which has been thus effected, has been due to different causes in different countries. In this country it has been chiefly promoted by the Parliament which, in the olden time, curbed the pretensions of a king, and which, almost in our own time, has limited the powers of an aristocracy. The history of the British Parliament has thus become identified with the history of the British people. Its growth has reflected their growth; its procedure their policy; its privileges their power. It is that growth, that procedure, and those privileges which it is the object of this book to describe.

A thousand years ago, when the Saxon still held supremacy in a united England, the wise men of the nation and the wise men of the shire were accustomed to meet and deliberate on affairs which affected the common weal. The Witenagemot—the assembly at which a nation sat in council—is thought by the best authorities to have been open to all the wise of the kingdom. But a popular gathering of this character tended from its very nature to become select. None but the wealthiest men could afford a journey which drew them from their families and their industry. By a natural process the meeting of the wise men became a meeting of great lords; and the summons of the king was limited to those whose attendance was alone probable. A few years after the Conquest, the Conqueror desired to imitate the example of his predecessors, and summoned a council of the noble and wise men of every county to consider what the customs of the kingdom were. This example was followed by his Norman successors. Bishops, abbots, earls, and barons, were occasionally summoned to the councils of the king. But the same reasons, which in Saxon times had limited the attendance of the majority of the people, interfered with the attendance of the lesser barons. Instead of coming themselves to the king's council, they deputed two or three of their number to represent them. This practice gradually led to a new custom. The bishops and greater barons were summoned by name. The sheriffs of each county were ordered to send representatives of the lesser barons or knights to the council of the king; and the new custom, in the course of time, received the sanction of written law. In signing the Great Charter, John promised to summon all archbishops, bishops, abbots, earls, and greater barons personally; and all other tenants in chief under the Crown by the sheriffs of their shires.

The Norman had endorsed the rule of the Saxon, and submitted to the necessity of parliamentary government. But forty years passed after the signature of the Great Charter before it was made plain that the representatives whom the sheriffs and bailiffs were to return were to be elected by the people, and not selected by the king's officer. In 1254 the sheriff was expressly directed to cause to come to the king's council two good and discreet knights of the county whom the men of the county shall have chosen for the purpose. The gradual progress of ideas had thus led to the constitution of a Parliament in which the greater barons were to serve in person, and the men of the county by their representatives. But, in the meanwhile, other changes were taking place in England which were preparing the way for a greater reform. Little communities were arising in different parts of the country, bent on plying the humble industries of their craft, and clinging together for the protection which their rural neighbours hoped to derive from their feudal lord. Free men in a free state, they prospered as free industry will always prosper; and, while the feudal Zähdarms around them were consuming their substance and killing their game, grew in influence and power. The most conspicuous character of the thirteenth century, Simon de Montfort, a Frenchman by birth, an Englishman by adoption, happened to require their aid to curb the pretensions of the greater barons with whose help he had struck down the power of Henry III. He gained the battle of Lewes; and followed up his victory by summoning a Parliament and by directing the sheriffs to return two knights for each county, and two burgesses for each borough in the kingdom. He was perhaps unconscious of the great change which his victory had promoted; he had laid the foundation of a House of Commons.

For a few years, indeed, the importance of the change which was thus effected was imperfectly understood both by king and people; and, in the Parliament of 1294, almost a generation after Lewes, the knights of the shires sat alone without any borough members. But, in the Parliament of the following year, the precedent which had been laid down by de Montfort was again followed. The sheriffs were directed to return two knights for each shire, two citizens for each city, and two burghers for each borough. From that time to this, the representatives of cities and boroughs uniformly sat with the knights of the shire; and with them formed the Commons' House of Parliament.

He is only a bad historian who traces the progress of events by the decisive battles of the world. The geologist pursues a better system, and does not confound the ruins of an eruption with the gradual growth of strata for countless ages. In the history of man, as in the history of nature, the main interest is concentrated on the progress of society, and not on the convulsions which have disturbed it. But, if men will persist in mistaking the victories of armies for the progress of society, let them at least rise from a contemplation of mere bloodshed to a consideration of results, and overlooking the Crecys and the Agincourts, by which provinces have been temporarily won or lost, weigh the consequences of such a victory as that which de Montfort gained at Lewes over Henry III.

The battle of Lewes had, in fact, insured the representation of urban as well as rural England in future Parliaments. More than two centuries had elapsed since the Conquest; and an event, which might possibly have led to the introduction of arbitrary government, had been gradually succeeded by the completion of representative institutions. But the results, which were thus secured, would perhaps have never ensued, if the Norman kings had not found themselves fettered by a want of money. The necessities of kings are the opportunities of peoples; and the truth never received a clearer and better illustration than in Norman and Plantagenet England. In Saxon times the Witenagemot had imposed extraordinary taxation. The earlier Norman kings probably levied their revenues without much consideration for the wishes of those who paid them. But even Henry I. described an aid as the gift of his barons; and, under the weaker hands of his successors, men ventured to refuse to pay aids which they had not personally voted. John, at Runnymede, distinctly undertook that no scutage or aid, save the three regular aids, should be henceforth imposed without the advice and consent of the national council; and, before the close of the thirteenth century, a wise statute framed in the reign of a wise king invested the Parliament, which had at last been fully constituted, with the sole power of taxation. The statute of 1297, which still remains on the statute book, commenced by declaring that no tallage or aid shall be taken without the good will and assent of archbishops, bishops, earls, barons, knights, burgesses, and other freemen of the land.

The statute of 1297 secured to Parliament the sole power of taxation. Prescription had already invested it with legislative powers. In Saxon England, the laws had undoubtedly been framed with the counsel and consent of the Witan; and the Norman kings, from the nature of their position, found themselves compelled to adopt the same procedure. The council to which the Conqueror entrusted the task of determining the customs or laws of the kingdom must have had legislative powers, since declaratory Acts of Parliament are nothing but laws. But, for more than two centuries, the germ of truth which could be detected in the Conqueror's reference to his council lay undeveloped and unfruitful. "In 1295, however, Edward I. transmuting" a mere legal maxim, "borrowed from Justinian," into a great political and constitutional principle, declared "that that which touches all shall be approved by all;" and in 1322 Parliament, under the weak rule of Edward II., gave the sanction of law to the wise dictum of Edward I. In a statute, which will be found printed in the supplement to the revised edition of the statutes, it was expressly declared that the matters which are to be established for the estate of our Lord the King, and of his heirs, and for the estate of the realm and of the people, shall be treated, accorded, and established in Parliament by our Lord the King, and by the consent of the prelates, earls, and barons and the commonalty of the realm according as it hath been heretofore accustomed.

The statute of 1322 had not altered the custom. It had merely given the sanction of law to the dictum of Edward I. and to the rule which had been usually observed both by the Conqueror and his successors. But this rule did not give Parliament the power of legislation. It merely provided that the king should not exercise his right of legislating without the assistance of the legislature. It admitted that the law was made by the king; and this admission has survived all the subsequent changes in the constitution to our own time. "Be it enacted by the Queen's most excellent Majesty, by and with the advice and consent of the Lords spiritual and temporal, and Commons in this present Parliament assembled," is the formula with which modern Acts of Parliament begin. The fact, however, that the king made the law, had frequently led to dangerous experiments. It was difficult to distinguish between an ordinance issued by the king in council, and a statute made by him with the advice of his Parliament. The magnates of Parliament were frequently members of the king's council. For two centuries after the Conquest the magnates alone had an undisputed right to parliamentary representation. Even a well-intentioned king might have failed to see any great distinction between an ordinance made on the advice of his wise men in council, and a statute made on the advice of the same men in Parliament. Some of the great bulwarks of English liberty are, indeed, ordinances and not statutes. It has been well observed by Mr. Stubbs that the assizes of Henry II. are ordinances; that Magna Charta was an ordinance; that Henry III., in confirming the charters, professed to act of his own spontaneous will; and it may be added that the great statute of Tallage purports to come direct from the Crown without the advice of either magnates or Parliament. Even after 1322 the king occasionally asserted his right to legislate. In October 1341, Edward III. ventured on repealing the laws which he had enacted on the petition of Parliament in the previous May. Richard II. had the arrogance to declare that the laws were in the mouth and breast of the king, and that he by himself could change and frame the laws of the kingdom. But these claims were never admitted by Parliament. The legislature in 1343 formally rescinded the statute which Edward III. had revoked in 1341, thereby ignoring the king's claim to repeal it without the advice of his Parliament; the deposition of Richard II. was voted by the Parliament which he had affected to supersede; and, after 1322, the legislature took care, in the case of every fresh enactment, to insert direct mention of its own authority. "Our sovereign lord King Edward that now is"—to cite one of the very first examples—"at his Parliament holden at Westminster by the common council of the prelates, earls, barons, and other great men, and of the commonalty of the realm, there being by his commandment, hath provided, ordered, and established in the form following."

The Parliament which was thus constituted comprised several distinct classes or estates of the community. The clergy formed one estate; the Lords another; the Commons a third; and each of these three estates, from the earliest period of which there is any record, deliberated in separate chambers apart. Separate sittings were obviously convenient. The circumstance, which usually led to the summoning of the estates, was the necessity for making provision for the Crown; and, as no tax was legal which was not conceded by those who paid it, the Lords voted their scutages and aids; the Commons their tenths and fifteenths; the clergy the higher taxes, which were paid by the revenues of the Church, apart. But the shape which the three estates ultimately assumed was only reached by a gradual process. In 1244, prelates, earls, and barons, all deliberated apart; a century afterwards it was still doubtful whether the knights of the shire would be ultimately merged with the Lords or with the Commons, and it has been suggested by Mr. Stubbs that, " as money was voted by the different estates in different proportions, possibly the prelates and clergy, the lords temporal, the knights of the shire, and the borough members may have sat in four companies and four chambers. The present arrangement, by which the lords spiritual and temporal sit in one house and the Commons in another, probably dates from about the middle of the fourteenth century. About the same time, the clergy gradually excused themselves from the cost and inconvenience of parliamentary attendance. They discovered that they could vote their taxes at the provincial convocations; and the Crown, which chiefly cared about obtaining their money, acquiesced in their non-attendance in Parliament. Long afterwards, in 1664, Convocation abandoned its right to tax the clergy. The three estates of the Crown thus gradually underwent an organic change. The clergy, Lords, and Commons were turned into the Lords spiritual, the Lords temporal, and the Commons.

This slight sketch of the progress of parliamentary institutions in England will show that the legislature only gradually assumed the form which it ultimately obtained. By a process of slow development the Witenagemot of the Saxon kings became the Parliament of modern England; and the three estates of the Crown ranged themselves in the two Houses of Lords and Commons. The close of the thirteenth century saw the accomplishment of the first of these results; the middle of the fourteenth century saw the conclusion of the second of them. Before the latter of these dates Parliament had obtained its modern name. The Witenagemot was an impossible term for an assembly whose members conversed in low Latin or in Norman-French. The council summoned by the Norman kings was sometimes known as a *colloquium*, and the modern name Parliament only came into use towards the close of the twelfth century. If it had not come into use at that time, the term probably would have never been applied to the legislature. French superseded Latin about the commencement of the fourteenth century. "Under Henry III.," writes Mr. Stubbs, "French had become the language of our written laws; under

Edward I. it appears as the language of the courts of law," and Edward II. took the coronation oath, not in Latin but in French. The word Parliament was obviously introduced into our language at the period when French was supplanting Latin. But the use of French—though it left a permanent impression on the English people— was only temporary. The earlier Plantagenets lost some of their continental possessions; the policy of the later Plantagenets separated the interests of England from those of France. France became the rival of England; and the victories of which the English were most proud were won over the French. An English literature was the natural result of the rise of England; and the kings who appealed to the English people paid them the compliment of speaking to them in their own language. In 1362—two years after the peace of Bretigny—English came into use in the law courts; and in 1365 Parliament was opened with an English speech. Some relics, however, both of French and Latin have survived till our own time. It is only in the last fifteen years that the use of Latin names for the days of the week has been abandoned in the record of proceedings of the House of Commons. Latin is still employed for this purpose by the House of Lords; and the Crown, when it assents to a bill, still uses the old Norman-French formula—a solitary survival of the language which was once commonly heard in Parliament.

It was long after Parliament acquired its modern name before it obtained a regular place of assembly. A council summoned to aid the king naturally met where the king happened to be staying. "Thrice a year," says the chronicler, " King William wore his crown every year that he was in England; at Easter he wore it at

Winchester, at Pentecost at Westminster, at Christmas at Gloucester." But the practice of the Conqueror in this respect was not followed by his successors. In addition to the three places at which the Conqueror wore his crown, councils or Parliaments were held by his successors at York, Northampton, Lincoln, Bury, Leicester, Coventry, Reading, Salisbury, Carlisle, Nottingham, Cambridge, Shrewsbury, Clarendon, Woodstock, and other places. Westminster, however, soon became the ordinary home of Parliament. The Lords generally sat in a room known as the King's Chamber or Painted Chamber. The Commons usually occupied the Chapter House of the Abbey, and only moved into St. Stephen's Chapel—a building which was to give Parliament itself a supplementary title—in the reign of the Tudors. The conveniences afforded by these buildings were probably greater than those available in the other cities and towns to which Parliament was summoned. And the situation of Westminster in southern England, its propinquity to capital and court, and its accessibility by the Thames conspired to make it the seat of government.

The councils and Parliaments which were thus held were summoned for some centuries at regular intervals. But a journey thrice a year to the king's court would have proved an insupportable burden to even wealthy men, and annual Parliaments were gradually substituted for assemblies thrice a year. This custom ultimately obtained the sanction of law, and in 1330 and 1362 statutes were passed enjoining the annual assembly of Parliament. During the fourteenth, and the first half of the fifteenth, century, the rule which was thus laid down was usually though not constantly obeyed. Kings, frequently spending more money than they possessed, could not, in fact, afford to dispense with the assistance of Parliaments; and the Parliaments, summoned to provide for the wants of sovereigns, were thus given frequent opportunities of redressing the grievances of the people. But, from the accession of the House of York, other counsels were adopted. Edward IV. was frugal in his expenditure, successful in his speculations, and arbitrary in his ideas of government. The civil war which had preceded his accession had seen the noblest heads in England fall, one after another, in battle or on the scaffold. The strength of the Lords was thus weakened or destroyed, the Commons alone had not sufficient influence to resist the Crown, and the king therefore, secure from the weakness of his subjects, was able to enforce his views of despotic government on the nation. Thus, from the accession of the House of York, a new period of English history commences. Up to that time the course of constitutional development, though frequently interrupted, had been on the whole continuous. From that time for a century and a half, England was the victim of more or less despotic governments.

From the accession of the House of York, Parliament was generally assembled at irregular intervals; the work of legislation was frequently interrupted by disturbances and civil war, and the necessity for taxation was partly superseded by the invention of benevolences, or loans, nominally granted to the sovereign by the benevolence or free will of the donor, but in reality exacted by the Crown. These three innovations—the interruption of Parliaments, the suspension of legislation, and the exaction of benevolences,—placed this country for a century and a half under the personal government of the Crown. After 1523 there was no Parliament for nearly seven years. Elizabeth was in this respect a greater offender than her father, and during the whole of her reign she continually dispensed for long periods with the services of a Parliament. The Tudor Parliaments usually acted with a subservience which might have won for them more consideration. In the reign of Henry VIII. Parliament enabled the king, after he had attained the age of twenty-four years, to repeal any statute passed since his accession to the throne. Shortly afterwards it vested the proclamations of the king in council with the force of legislation. The constitutional historian may find room for congratulation that the power thus transferred to the king was conceded to him by the legislature. The result was, in any case, the same. The substance of authority was yielded to the king. The shadow of it was retained by the Parliament.

It may, perhaps, be thought that the power which was thus grasped by the Crown was productive of few inconveniences. Parliament, indeed, resumed under Edward VI. the powers which it had conceded to his father; and, from that time forward, the legislative authority nominally remained with the legislature. But the privileges which one monarch obtains by regular processes, is grasped by another irregularly; and Elizabeth, imitating her father's example, and neglecting even to obtain the sanction of her Parliaments, claimed what Hallam has called "a supplemental right of legislation." The queen's proclamations dealt with the most varied subjects—the banishment of Anabaptists, the cultivation of woad, the exportation of corn, the regulation of wearing apparel, the growth of London. But wise and unwise, important and unimportant, these proclamations were all branded with the same mark. They all asserted the right of the Crown to regulate matters which, in earlier times, the legislature had scrupulously reserved for its own treatment. The great constitutional principles, which had been slowly elaborated in Plantagenet England, were forgotten and ignored in Tudor times; and, in matters of legislation, England had virtually fallen into a condition of personal government.

This result was, in itself, sufficiently formidable. It was made much more serious in consequence of the power, which the Crown claimed, to dispense with the aid of Parliament in matters of taxation. Benevolences, the intolerable invention of Edward IV., had been declared illegal by a statute of Richard III. But it was supposed that the latter statute did not prohibit the grant of voluntary gifts to the Crown; and, with clever management, it became impossible to distinguish between the voluntary gift and the enforced exaction. In the reign of Henry VII. Archbishop Morton propounded the famous fork which has preserved his memory, but which compelled both rich and poor to submit to the illegal exactions of his master. In the reign of Henry VIII. Wolsey raised illegal taxation to a science, and issued commissions for levying a sixth part of each man's substance. The disturbances, which these unprecedented demands occasioned, forced Wolsey to give way; and gave Shakespeare an excuse for assuming that the exaction was the minister's, the concession the king's:

> " Have you a precedent
> Of this commission? I believe not any.
> We must not rend our subjects from our laws,
> And stick them in our will."

Yet those who are best acquainted with English history will be the first to reject the charitable interpretation which Shakespeare has placed on Henry's conduct. In despotic periods, ministers adapt their policy to the wishes of their masters. Under Henry VII. Morton invented his fork; under Henry VIII. Wolsey attempted his exactions; under Mary a duty on foreign cloth was imposed without the authority of the legislature; under Elizabeth a similar duty, equally unauthorized, was imposed on foreign wine.

A king who exercises independently the right of taxation and the right of legislation, is virtually despotic; and, for the 120 years during which the Tudors reigned, England was under a despotic form of government. It is hardly necessary to observe that despotism became possible from the great ability of the sovereigns who successively occupied the throne. But even Henry VII., Henry VIII., and Elizabeth would not have maintained their position if it had not been for the weakness of their opponents. During the whole period, indeed, the aristocracy and the people were gradually recovering from the prostrate condition to which long years of civil warfare had consigned them. The peerage, recruited by fresh additions to its numbers, and enriched by the confiscation of the abbey lands, in a manner which will be shown in the succeeding chapter, was gaining fresh strength. The Commons were accurately reflecting the growing power which the community in general was deriving from the increase of wealth. The Tudors, to do them bare justice, kept order; and the prosperity, which order promoted, was preparing the forces which were to overwhelm Tudor despotism. Thus it happened that the conditions under which

Elizabeth ruled were widely different from those under which her father and grandfather acted. Henry VII. succeeded in establishing, and Henry VIII. was enabled to maintain, a personal monarchy because they were confronted by no forces strong enough to resist them. Elizabeth accomplished the harder task of preserving the autocracy which she had found by the wisdom of her rule and the lightness of her burdens. Henry VIII. could venture to be prodigal; Elizabeth was compelled to be frugal. The people, secured under her firm rule, were dazzled by their own prosperity. Cultured England was gratified by the production of literary works of the highest genius; commercial England was consoled by the vast expansion of industry and trade; and the common people, conscious of their own welfare, were contented with their lot. The nation saw that it was prosperous, and forgot that it was no longer free.

A despotism of this kind was perhaps more fatal to liberty than the autocracy established by Henry VII. Under the 7th and 8th Henries the people could see the sword of the oppressor; under Elizabeth they could only see the rich scabbard in which it was sheathed. If the Virgin Queen could have obtained immortality it might have been with England as it was with France. But personal government was shaken by her death; it fell never to rise again with the head of Charles I. upon the scaffold at Whitehall. The Stuarts, indeed, were at least as capable men as the majority of the monarchs who had preceded them. It has been said by a high authority that Charles II. was "the last king of England who was a man of parts," and his unfortunate father and pedantic grandfather had ability like their descendant. The Stuarts, moreover, came to

England with views of government at least as despotic as those which had been embraced by the Tudors. In the eye of James monarchy was the true pattern of divinity; the king was above the law; and passive obedience was the sole duty of his subjects. The Church and the Bench supported the view which the king promulgated; and the duty of obedience was enforced in the courts of law on the week days and preached from the pulpits on the Sundays.

But the position of James was widely different from that of Elizabeth. The forces by which the Crown was controlled were daily acquiring strength. The king was a stranger to his new subjects, with Scotch and French blood mixing in his veins; his title was, in the eyes of many people, doubtful; his virtues were the mere virtues of a pedant; his vices were vices "*quæ versu dicere non est.*" Yet this king played in England the part which Rehoboam had played in Israel. The three innovations, which had been introduced by the Tudors, were government for long intervals without a Parliament, the issue of proclamations unwarranted by statute, the exaction of taxation without the consent of the legislature. All these three devices were employed by the Stuarts; and Parliament was rarely summoned when its assembly could be avoided, and seldom assembled without being insulted. The infrequent Parliaments of Stuart times were, however, engaged in one long struggle with the Crown. The first Parliament of James's reign incurred the anger of the king by boldly remonstrating on many occasions against the grievances which the people endured. The second Parliament of James, summoned after a seven years' interval, vainly repeating the complaints of its predecessor, was dissolved without passing a single bill. His third Parliament revived the right of impeachment, and avenged the arrest of a member by a protestation of its liberties. His fourth and last Parliament abolished monopolies, and complained of the proclamations which the king had issued. The first Parliament of Charles insisted on a redress of grievances before it settled a permanent supply on the Crown. His second Parliament was memorable for the impeachment of the Duke of Buckingham, and for the arrest of Sir John Eliot and Sir Dudley Digges for words spoken in derogation of the king's honour. His third Parliament drew up the great Petition of Right, to which the king gave a reluctant assent. His fourth Parliament, after only a few days' session, was dissolved, and succeeded by the fifth Parliament, which commenced the Civil War.

James and Charles would, in fact, have dispensed with parliamentary assistance altogether if they had been able to enforce their proclamations and collect the arbitrary taxes which they imposed. But, soon after the commencement of the reign of James, three judges, on the advice of Coke, decided that proclamations unauthorised by statute could not be enforced; and the various devices to which the Stuarts successively resorted for raising money one after another failed. The minor expedients which they employed for this purpose were the sale of monopolies and the sale of honours. The first of these was declared illegal; the second was a source of revenue which from its very nature was only limited. The Stuarts, therefore, like the Tudors, had to fall back upon arbitrary taxation, and their exactions took the form of benevolences and forced loans, of duties on merchandise, and of ship-money. Arbitrary taxation, however, proved difficult of collection. The benevolence, which James imposed after the dissolution of his second Parliament, was resisted by Mr. Oliver St. John, whose contumacy was punished in the Star Chamber by a fine of £5,000 and an imprisonment during pleasure. The loan which Charles I. levied in 1625 was extensively resisted, and many persons, among whom Hampden was one, were thrown into custody for refusing to pay it. The Crown experienced a similar resistance in its attempt to enforce other taxation. Bates, a Turkey merchant, declined to pay a duty of 5s. per hundredweight imposed on currants. The Commons, in James's first Parliament, remonstrated on the publication of a book of rates—or customs' duties on merchandise—arbitrarily imposed by the Crown. In Charles's reign, Chambers, a sturdy Puritan, incurred imprisonment rather than pay an illegal duty on foreign silk; and shortly afterwards Hampden earned the undying gratitude of his fellow-countrymen by resisting the payment of ship-money. It has been reserved to a modern statesman to declare that a "virtuous and able monarch" was "martyred because, among other benefits projected for his people, he was of opinion that it was more for their advantage that the economic service of the state should be supplied by direct taxation levied by an individual known to all, than by indirect taxation raised by an irresponsible and fluctuating assembly." Lord Beaconsfield, however, had an hereditary incapacity to understand the history of the seventeenth century. The issue in 1634 was not, of course, whether taxation should be direct or indirect. The imprisonment of Hampden had been preceded by the imprisonment of Chambers. The issue was far greater. It settled for ever whether England should be enslaved or free.

Thus the parliamentary history of England, from the earliest times to the death of Charles I., is roughly divisible into three periods. During the first period Parliament was acquiring shape and power; during the second period the Crown was endeavouring to establish an autocratic authority; during the third period the Parliament was regaining the position which it had lost during the second. The history of England from the assembly of the Long Parliament to the present time is of a different character. Throughout the whole period the authority of Parliament was virtually supreme. Amidst the crash of civil war, indeed, the legislature was occasionally controlled by brute force. The restored Stuarts endeavoured on more than one occasion to return to the system which the first James and the first Charles had pursued. The dispensing power which James II. claimed, and the declaration for liberty of conscience which he issued, involved the suspension of statutes which Parliament had passed. But the fate of Charles I. made any serious attempt in that direction impracticable. Kings might still dream of the autocracy of the Tudors; their flatterers might still talk of the divine right of monarchs. The headsman's axe had made dreams and flattery purposeless, and had superseded the right divine by parliamentary government.

Even the slight sketch in the foregoing pages has been probably sufficient to emphasize the three measures by which Tudors and Stuarts had endeavoured to establish autocracy in this country: (1) They had convened Parliament at irregular and distant intervals; (2) They had superseded the statutes of Parliament by proclamations of their own; and (3) They had taxed the people without the assent of Parliament. The last Parliament of Charles I. endeavoured to prevent the repetition of the first of these three evils. It passed an act, known in history as the Triennial Act, which declared that a new Parliament should always be summoned within three years of the dissolution of an old one. This Act rendered it impossible for any monarch to dispense with a Parliament for long periods of time. The same Parliament declared ship-money illegal, and prohibited the unauthorised levying of customs on merchandise. The machinery by which Tudors and Stuarts had endeavoured to supplant their legislatures was in this way taken from them. A king, forced to summon a Parliament at least once in three years, and unable to levy a tax without parliamentary authority, would, it was supposed, have little chance of establishing a system of personal government.

This reasoning, however, was exposed to one fatal objection. The innovations, which Tudor and Stuart had made, had been introduced in direct defiance of the law, and it was obviously as easy for future monarchs to disobey the statutes of the Long Parliament as it had been for Henry or Elizabeth to disregard the rules of the Great Charter or the laws of the Plantagenets. The two sovereigns, with whose rule England was cursed after the Restoration, showed that they had every disposition to imitate, so far as they dared, their father's example. The attitude of the later Stuarts, indeed, differed in a striking manner from that of the earlier Stuarts. The first James and first Charles claimed the force of law for their proclamations; the duty of obedience to their commands for ship-money. The second Charles and second James were mainly interested in asserting their right to dispense with the operation of certain penal statutes. The proclamations and exactions of the first Stuarts brought them into collision with the legislature. The dispensing power of the later Stuarts brought them into collision with the Church; and thus arose the striking difference that, while at the Rebellion prominent churchmen were on the side of the Crown, prominent churchmen at the Revolution were on the side of the people. The claim, however, both of the former and of the later Stuarts was founded on the same inadmissible pretensions which placed the Crown above the law; and the legislature learning wisdom from experience decided like the Psalmist to put not its trust in princes any longer. There were two things which the circumstances of England required—a military force, and money to support it. Parliament gave the Crown the power which it required for controlling an army, but it limited the power to a year. It gave the Crown the necessary supplies for its support, but it gave them only for twelve months. It had at last found a better method than even Magna Charta and the Petition of Right for asserting its own supremacy. It could even in future put its trust in princes, for it had made its princes powerless to break their faith.

Since that time a Triennial Act and a Septennial Act have been passed; but the new Acts did not provide against long intervals without a Parliament, but against any Parliament being allowed to survive for more than three or seven years. The old Triennial Act of Charles I. was a weapon forged by Parliament against the Crown. The Triennial Act of William III. and the Septennial

Act of George I. were intended to prevent the subserviency of Parliaments. The first Triennial Act strengthened the control of Parliament over the Crown. The second strengthened the control of the people over Parliament. The measures which have been adopted almost in our own time to make this control real must be reserved for future treatment in subsequent chapters. In this chapter it has been only possible to trace the steps which placed England under a limited monarchy and which made Parliament virtually though not nominally supreme.

CHAPTER II.

THE HOUSE OF LORDS.

THE attempt, which has been made in the preceding chapter to sketch the prominent facts in the early history of Parliament, cannot claim the merit of a finished picture. A bare outline is the utmost which it is possible to draw in a book of this character; and the student who desires more detailed information must necessarily turn to the more elaborate works on which the preceding account is mainly founded. Enough, however, has perhaps been written to show how the various classes of the community gradually grouped themselves into three estates, and how the three estates ultimately ranged themselves into two houses. Of these houses, the House of Commons has the greater interest for the student of modern history. Its struggles have been the nation's struggles; its growth has reflected the nation's growth; its victories have secured the nation's liberties. But the antiquarian, or the historian, derives as much or greater interest from tracing the history of the House of Lords. The antiquarian regards it as the representative of the Witenagemot of his forefathers: the historian recollects that it fought the battle of English liberty when the Commons were either unrepresented or powerless. Every liberal Englishman now founds his hopes on the Commons; but the most liberal Englishman may thank God that in the olden time there was a House of Lords.

Mr. Freeman is the historian who has most strenuously insisted on the resemblance which the House of Lords of to-day bears to the Witenagemot of the eleventh century. According to this high authority the House of Lords may fairly claim that it is the legitimate descendant of the ancient Witenagemot. Yet the difference between the old and the modern assembly is as' great as that between the modern peer and the Saxon earl or the Norman baron. The Witenagemot was nominally an assembly of the men of the nation. In practice it was really a meeting of the *witan* or wise men. The wisdom of Saxon, as of other times, was generally gauged by the extent of a man's property, the position which he occupied, or the favour of the Crown. In the Witenagemot the ealdormen of Saxon England represented property; the prelates and greater abbots, position; the king's thegns, favour. The Witenagemot rarely included a hundred members, and the king's thegns formed frequently a majority of the whole. The assembly which was thus composed exercised both legislative and judicial powers. In theory it controlled the king; in practice it frequently registered the wishes of the sovereign, to whom the majority of its members owed their presence at its deliberations. It was inevitable that such an assembly should undergo a process of modification when the Conquest and the conquerors introduced feudal ideas into the conquered country. Bishops, abbots, and earls still attended its meetings. But they attended not in virtue of the king's summons, but as the king's tenants-in-chief. In strict feudal theory, all the king's tenants-in-chief were entitled to be present at his council. The earl, the bishop, and the abbot were summoned not in virtue of their wisdom nor of their position, but on account of their estates; and the character of the assembly was modified in consequence. This change naturally introduced a new rank into the peerage: earl, prelate, and abbot all sat as in Saxon times; but the barons, who were neither earls nor churchmen, were also admitted to the council. The earl was originally the ealdorman of the county, and the earliest ealdormen all derived their titles from counties or county towns. But the baron or king's man—for the word baron only means a man—was simply the king's tenant or vassal, who owed his seat to his relations with the king, his feudal lord.

In theory, then, the council of the Norman kings consisted of his vassals or tenants-in-chief. In practice only the greater barons were summoned to the assembly. The minor barons, too poor to bear the cost of attendance at court, readily submitted to their own exclusion; and the council, instead of consisting of all the barons by tenure, was thus limited to the baronies whose representatives in successive generations were summoned by the king's writs to attend. By the close of the thirteenth century a baronage by tenure had been virtually superseded, so far as lay peers were concerned, by an hereditary peerage created by summons. Almost a century afterwards, Richard II. made the first Lord Beauchamp baron by letters-patent; and the precedent was thus formed for the modern method of creating peerages.

In the meanwhile, however, other innovations of more

social but less constitutional importance had been introduced into the peerage. The greatest men in the state, with that strange appetite for rank which seems as insatiable among the rich as it is incomprehensible to ordinary minds, were not satisfied with the old Saxon title of earl or the Norman title of baron. Edward III. made his eldest son in 1337, his younger sons in 1362, dukes. In the following reigns some of the greatest subjects were dignified with titles which had originally been introduced to gratify the cravings of men of royal birth; and the intermediate title of markgrave, margrave, or marquis was at the same time imported from the Continent to reward other subjects only slightly less distinguished than those on whom dukedoms were conferred. Two more generations passed before an Englishman was found who preferred the strange unmeaning title of viscount to the Norman barony.

During the greater portion of the period under review the number of peers summoned to Parliament was a diminishing quantity. Mr. Stubbs has observed that eleven earls and ninety-eight barons were summoned to the Parliament of 1300. "The average number of barons," he says elsewhere, "summoned to a full Parliament by Edward II. was seventy-four; the average of the reign of Edward III. was forty-three." At the commencement of the reign of Henry IV. the lay members of the House of Lords consisted of four dukes, one marquis, ten earls, and thirty-four barons. The forfeitures arising from the civil Wars of the Roses effectually prevented the further growth of the temporal peerage, and the lay lords rarely exceeded fifty in number till after the accession of the House of Tudor. They dwindled to forty-four in 1461, and to thirty-four in

1470. This diminution in the number of the peers limited the influence of the lay peerage; and the diminution had an additional significance because it was not accompanied by a corresponding decrease in the number of the other members of the House of Lords. Two archbishops and eighteen bishops regularly sat in the Upper House; and the heads of twenty-seven great religious houses were uniformly summoned to it from the reign of Edward III. to Tudor times. The ecclesiastical element in Parliament was therefore represented by a permanent body of forty-seven individuals. Even in the thirteenth and fourteenth centuries the spiritual peers formed a considerable minority. In the fifteenth century they became the majority of the chamber. It must be recollected that the twenty-seven parliamentary abbots were elected by monks who probably paid more allegiance to Rome than to England; and that the twenty prelates, nominally elected by the chapters, were virtually appointed by the Pope on the nomination of the Crown. The hereditary peerage, therefore, formed a minority in the House of Lords; and the majority of the House was more or less under papal influence. The contest between Rome and England, which was kindled into activity in the reign of Henry II., and which culminated in the Statute of Provisors in the reign of Edward III., was a political and not a religious contest; and the liberties of England, for which the House of Lords was at that time the chief bulwark, were imperilled by the influence which the Crown derived from its alliance with Rome, and from the dwindling numbers of the hereditary peerage.

The Wars of the Roses, and the exhaustion of the nobility, placed England, at the close of the fifteenth century, at the mercy of the Tudors. Parliament proved unable to withstand the power of the Crown; and, for a century and a half, England was under the personal rule of Tudor and Stuart. It has been already stated, in the previous chapter, that the forces with which the Crown was confronted gradually increased in power; and this remark is especially true of the lay members of the House of Lords. The lay element of the House of Lords was strengthened, directly, by the additions which were made to its numbers; and indirectly, but still more effectually, by the removal from it of the heads of the great monasteries. Henry VII. only summoned 29 lay peers to his first Parliament. The greatest number summoned by Henry VIII. was 51; 82 peers sat in the first Parliament of James I., and 96 in his last; Charles summoned 117 peers to the Parliament of 1628, and 119 to that of 1640. Additions of this kind, small as they seem to a modern reader, accustomed to the lavish bestowal of dignities by recent ministers, increased the numbers of the peerage and strengthened the influence of the peers. But the dissolution of the monasteries had a still more important effect. "Though the number of abbots and priors," wrote Hallam, "to whom writs of summons were directed, varied considerably in different Parliaments, they always, joined to the twenty-one bishops, preponderated over the temporal peers." The dissolution of the monasteries changed this condition. The lay members of the House of Lords—hitherto a powerless minority—were converted at one stroke into a majority of the Upper House of Parliament.

The political effects of this revolution—the greatest which had occurred up to that time in the English

Parliament—have attracted insufficient notice from most historians. Occupied with the great religious change which was almost simultaneously effected, they have dwelt at only an inadequate length on the altered conditions which the House of Lords thenceforward assumed. But the change did more even in a mere political sense than convert a minority into a majority. It strengthened the lay peers as they had never been strengthened before. The vast estates which the abbots and priors enjoyed were lavishly distributed among the nobility and gentry of the kingdom; and many of the greatest families of the present day owe their wealth and possessions to the spoils of a Church with which Henry rewarded their ancestors. "Something like a fifth of the actual land in the kingdom," writes Mr. Green, "was in this way transferred from the holding of the Church to that of nobles and gentry. Not only were the older houses enriched, but a new aristocracy was erected from among the dependants of the court. The Russells, Cavendishes, and Fitzwilliams are familiar instances of families which rose from obscurity through the enormous grants of Church land made to Henry's courtiers. The old baronage was hardly crushed before a new aristocracy took its place." Neither king nor minister appreciated the consequences of their own acts. They were only eager to purchase support for the policy of the hour. They failed to see that they were forging a weapon which was ultimately to overthrow personal government in this country.

For nearly a century after the dissolution of the monasteries, these conditions remained unchanged. The lay members of the peerage increased in number, in wealth, and in influence; and the encroachments continually made by the Crown forced all classes of the laity into alliance. In Stuart times, however, the Church —or at any rate the bishops who represented the Church—showed an increasing disposition to support the pretensions of the Crown; while the bulk of the nation, moving steadily towards Puritanism, was regarding Episcopacy with indifference or dislike. These two circumstances naturally influenced the House of Commons; and, on the eve of the Civil War, a bill passed the Commons which was ultimately accepted by the Lords, excluding the bishops from the right to parliamentary attendance. In revolutions, the calmest minds are hurried on with a rapidity from which prudence recoils, and to extremes which reason disapproves. The peers had themselves assented, on the eve of the war, to the exclusion of the bishops from their councils. Their own extinction was voted at the close of it by the rump of a House of Commons.

The course of constitutional history had been rudely interrupted by the violent innovations of Tudors and Stuarts and the retributory measures of the Long Parliament. The waters had overflowed their banks, and the old landmarks had been hidden by the flood. But the flood subsided after the Restoration of 1660; and, though for another generation new dangers seemed frequently possible, the waters resumed their old channel and their course of steady progress after the Revolution. 139 peers were summoned to the first Parliament of Charles II. At the close of his reign the roll of the Lords comprised 176 names. The roll was increased to 192 peerages before the death of William III.; to 209 peerages before the death of Anne; to 216 peerages before the death of George I.; to 229 before the death of George II.; to 339 at the death of George III.; to 396 before the death of George IV.; to 456 at the death of William IV.; and to 512 in 1881. To put the same thing in another way, the peerage was increased by sixteen peerages in the seventeen years which elapsed from the death of Charles II. to the death of William III., or by about one peerage a year; by seventeen peerages in the twelve years of Anne's reign, or by nearly a peerage and a half a year; by twenty peerages in the thirty-seven years of George I. and George II., or by about one peerage in two years; by 110 peerages in the sixty years of George III., or by nearly two peerages a year; by fifty-seven peerages in the ten years of George IV., or by nearly six peerages a year; by sixty peerages in the reign of William IV., or by eight peerages and a half a year; and by fifty-six peerages in the forty-four years during which the Queen has reigned, or by a peerage and a quarter a year. The return is, of course, affected by the addition of representative peers for Scotland in the reign of Anne, and for Ireland in the reign of George III.; and to a lesser degree by the removal of the Irish spiritual peers in the present reign. But it will give, as it stands, an approximate idea of the growth of the British peerage. It ought, perhaps, also to be added that the increase during the present reign has occurred wholly during the last sixteen years. The first twenty-eight years of the Queen's reign saw no addition to the numbers of the House of Lords, since an old peerage, on an average, became extinct for every new peerage that was created by Her Majesty.

In the days when these additions to the number of the peerage were still small, they were regarded with

jealousy by the general public; and the reasons for this
jealousy are easily explicable. In the first place, the
House of Lords possessed a power of which it now only
retains the shadow. At the beginning of the eighteenth
century a great statesman who accepted a peerage lost
neither popularity nor influence. Towards the close of
the eighteenth century a peerage and a pension deprived
him, whom men loved to call the Great Commoner,
of more than half his power. In the next place, the
creation of a dozen peerages in the reign of Anne had
a different significance from their creation eighty years
afterwards. The larger the House of Lords became, the
smaller was the actual effect of a new peerage. These
two reasons—the importance of the House of Lords as
a deliberative assembly, and the vast influence which
the creation of new peers produced on its counsels,
made men in the first half of the eighteenth century
naturally jealous of large additions to the peerage. The
simultaneous creation of a dozen peers during the
administration of Harley gave point to this feeling;
and, in 1718, Sunderland introduced a bill to authorise
the Crown to create six new peers of England; to
substitute twenty-five hereditary peers of Scotland for
sixteen elective peers; but to forbid any further enlarge-
ment of the peerage. The bill passed the House of
Lords, but was rejected by the Commons chiefly through
Walpole's exertions. "Among the Romans," so Walpole
began his speech against the bill, "the temple of fame
was placed behind the temple of virtue, to denote that
there was no coming to the temple of fame but through
that of virtue. But, if this bill is passed into a law,
one of the most powerful incentives to virtue would
be taken away, since there would be no arriving at

honour but through the winding sheet of an old decrepit lord, or the grave of an extinct noble family." Perhaps few passages in any language could be quoted which prove more clearly the alteration of ideas through the progress of society. Manliness, which the old Romans called virtue, was a very different quality from that which even Walpole's audience would have regarded as virtue. The position which Walpole described as honour was becoming a mere refuge for wealth. The English temple of fame was becoming, in fact, the one place in England where it was difficult for a young man ambitious of honour to acquire distinction.

Yet, if Sunderland's bill had become law, the House of Lords must necessarily have perished. A limited oligarchy in an expanding community, it would, in the words of the Long Parliament, have become "useless and dangerous"; and its abolition would have been a matter of necessity. It was saved from almost immediate extinction by Walpole's opposition; the House of Lords, instead of remaining a limited body in a growing nation, grew with the nation's growth, and in some sort reflected the nation's progress. The unsparing use, which George III. made of his prerogative by the creation of an unprecedented number of peerages, is said by Mr. Buckle to have "laid the foundation for that disrepute into which since then the peers have been constantly falling." It may be doubted whether Mr. Buckle's judgment on this point is accurate. The complaint, indeed, which he made of George III.'s peers had been made by Selden of the peers of an earlier period. "The Lords that are ancient we honour, because we know not whence they come; but the new ones we slight, because we know their beginning." Defoe afterwards said the same thing in stronger language:

> " Wealth, howsoever got, in England makes
> Lords of mechanics, gentlemen of rakes.
> Antiquity and birth are needless here:
> 'Tis impudence and money make the peer.
> * * * * * *
> Great families of yesterday we show;
> And lords whose parents were the Lord knows who."

The wealthy nonentities on whom George III. bestowed peerages conferred little lustre on the assembly which they joined, but they brought it at least into harmony with the ruling classes of the nation. England at that time was virtually under the control of a small oligarchy of borough-owners. The most powerful borough-owners naturally stipulated for their own promotion to the House of Lords; and a large section of the House of Commons reflected the views of the noble patrons to whom they owed their political existence. George III.'s peerages, therefore, secured harmony between the two Houses,—the oligarchs and their representatives; and throughout his reign and that of his eldest son this harmony was undisturbed. The peers during the whole of this period were only a little more illiberal than the Commons. The true cause which brought the peerage into disrepute was not the lavish creations of George III., but the termination of government by an oligarchy. The amiable senators who constituted the Upper House of Parliament stood at last before the public without extraneous support. They had ceased to be borough owners and they were only peers.

The constant addition to the roll of the House of

Lords had a marked influence on the fortunes of the Church of England. In Plantagenet times the clergy had formed a separate estate of the Crown. In Tudor times the Lords Spiritual had formed the majority of the Upper House of Parliament. Even after the dissolution of the monasteries the twenty-six bishops had formed a compact and important minority of the Lords. But every successive addition to the peerage reduced, of course, the relative weight of the bishops' votes. The twenty-six bishops formed one-eighth of the Upper House in the days of Charles II. They comprise only one-twentieth of the Upper House at the present time. The episcopate, indeed, has of late years been slightly increased, but the addition to it has not been allowed to make any alteration in the number of the lords. It is true that Conservative statesmen, only forty years ago, could not understand an English bishop who was not a peer; and, when the necessity arose for providing new bishops for the populous dioceses of Ripon and Manchester, it was proposed to combine the old sees of Gloucester and Bristol, and of St. Asaph and Bangor, and so make room for the new bishops. The pride or the prejudice of the Welsh, however, resisted the union of Welsh sees, and it became consequently necessary to create a twenty-seventh bishopric. But the Administration did not venture on proposing the addition of a twenty-seventh spiritual peer, and it was arranged that the junior bishop—provided that he did not represent one of the great sees of London, Durham, and Winchester—should be excluded from Parliament. The same course has since been followed on the formation of new sees at St. Alban's, Truro, and Liverpool; the four junior bishops are spared the labours of parliamentary attendance, and their dioceses derive the advantage which ought to ensue from their attendance to their immediate duties, instead of spending the most valuable portion of the year in the irrelevant occupations of the House of Lords and the secular pursuits of a London season.

Yet the bishops in Parliament—out of place as they seem—represent a tradition and a principle. The eorl is hardly recognisable in the modern earl; the baron no longer sits by tenure; the presence of princes, dukes, marquises, and viscounts testifies to the innovations of the Plantagenets. The bishops alone preserve their almost unbroken descent from the days when the Witan of our Saxon ancestors gave counsels to the king. Their presence, moreover, reminds us that one section of the House of Lords has from time immemorial owed its position in Parliament to some other principle than birth. Lord Palmerston, in his first ministry, endeavoured to extend the principle by conferring a peerage for life on a distinguished lawyer; but the clamour which the proposal excited forced the Government to give way, and to confer an hereditary peerage in the ordinary manner on the gentleman who had been selected for the exceptional distinction. No Government has since attempted to fabricate life peerages on its own responsibility; but, in re-modelling the final Court of Appeal, the Legislature has quietly decided that two of the judges appointed to it may hold peerages for life.

The House of Lords, then, consists of two classes, the Lords spiritual and the Lords temporal. The Lords spiritual consist of the two archbishops, the three bishops of London, Durham, and Winchester, and twenty-one other English and Welsh bishops in the order of their seniority. The Lords temporal comprise the peers of the United Kingdom, who sit by virtue of descent; the representative peers of Ireland and Scotland, who sit by virtue of election; and the two life peers of the High Court of Appeal. The Lords spiritual sit in virtue of their office; the Lords temporal sit by descent, by creation, or by election. The Crown may create an indefinite number of new peerages, and the Whig ministry of 1830 obtained a pledge from William IV. that he would create peerages sufficient to ensure the passage of the Reform Act. Peers are usually created by letters-patent conferring the dignity on its recipient and his heirs male. But their creation is also occasionally effected by writ, or by a letter from the Crown, summoning the new peer to attend the House of Lords. The former course is uniformly adopted in the case of new peerages; the latter is usually pursued when the eldest son of a peer is summoned by one of his father's titles to sit in the House of Lords. The sixteen representative peers of Scotland are summoned for each Parliament; the twenty-eight representative peers of Ireland are summoned for life; the two life-peers, members of the High Court of Appeal, sit also for life.

At the beginning of the present year the House of Lords comprised 5 princes of the blood, 2 archbishops, 21 dukes, 19 marquises, 118 earls, 25 viscounts, 24 bishops, 254 barons, 28 representative peers of Ireland, and 16 representative peers of Scotland, or 512 peers. But this list embraces only the titles by which the peers hold their seats, and has no reference to the higher dignities which some of them enjoy as Scotch or Irish peers. The Duke of Abercorn sits as a marquis; the Dukes of Athole, Buccleuch, Montrose, and Roxburgh as earls; the Duke of Leinster as a viscount; and the Duke of Argyll as a baron. The Scotch and Irish titles, by which these men are popularly known, confer no right of admission to the House of Lords; and they sit there by the inferior dignities conferred upon them in the peerage of the United Kingdom. Since the Union with Scotland the Crown has been unable to create a new Scotch peerage; many Scotch peerages have naturally become extinct; the possessors of many others have had English dignities conferred upon them, and there are now only twenty-four peers of Scotland who do not sit in the British Parliament either as peers of England or as representative peers. With some inconsistency a different policy was pursued at the time of the Union with Ireland, and the Crown was empowered to create one Irish peerage for every three peerages that became extinct. Partly in consequence of this circumstance, there are still seventy-four Irish peers who have no seat in the House of Lords; and there are, therefore, ninety-eight peerages of Scotland and Ireland whose possessors have no direct right of their own, and no indirect right as the representatives of their order, to share in the deliberations of the Upper House of Parliament.

The House of Peers has inherited from the earliest ages a double duty. It is the Supreme Court of Appeal, and it is a branch of the legislature. The appellate jurisdiction of the peers will naturally be considered in another volume of this series. Their legislative functions will be more properly described in a later chapter of this volume. But the peers, as hereditary legislators, enjoy certain distinct privileges which ought to be mentioned at the present time. As hereditary counsellor to the Crown, each peer has a right of access to the throne; and examples may be found in which individual peers have had the assurance to tender advice to the sovereign in opposition to the opinions of his responsible ministers. In his legislative capacity, each peer has the right of recording his reasons for protesting against any decision on which the peers collectively agree; till very lately he had the right, instead of personally attending the debates, to place his proxy in the hands of a brother peer. The former privilege, which still survives, has led to a very remarkable series of short state papers. The latter privilege, which was quietly surrendered a dozen years ago, produced lax attendance and inattention to debate, thereby increasing the disrepute into which the Lords would under any circumstances have fallen. When the proxy of a noble lord discharging his official duties at Dublin, St. Petersburg, or Calcutta, who had neither heard the arguments addressed to the House, nor was even acquainted with the subject before it, was of equal value with that of the peer who was present, a new light was thrown on the doctrine of heredity. Even the stoutest Tories could not prove that a gentleman 3,000 miles off was entitled to decide issues of immediate interest to their fellow-countrymen at home.

These three privileges—the right of access to the throne, the right of voting by proxy, the right of protest—are the most important of those which have been enjoyed by the peers. But, in addition to these, the peers enjoy other privileges which require enumeration. The most important of these relate to their freedom from arrest in civil cases, and to their trial for treason or felony. Both of these privileges, which at first sight appear strange and indefensible, are easily explicable. (1) The public has a primary right to the attendance of the members of the legislature. No member of either House of Parliament can consequently be arrested on a civil case; and the person of the peer is for ever sacred and inviolable, because the House to which he belongs is never dissolved. (2) In cases of treason and felony peers can only be tried by their peers; but this rule, apparently so indefensible, is only an extension of the old rule which gives every accused person the advantage of a jury of his equals. The peers of a peer are necessarily peers. Many people who are still alive can recollect the trial of the late Lord Cardigan, for shooting Captain Tuckett in a duel, in accordance with this rule. But the incidents of this trial, and the acquittal of Lord Cardigan on a technical issue of only minor importance, did not reconcile the country to the revival of an antiquated and cumbrous tribunal.

Such is the history, such are the privileges of the House of Lords. The antiquary regards it as the hereditary descendant of the Witenagemot of our Saxon ancestors; the historian associates it with some of the most memorable scenes of English history; the statesman recollects with gratitude that its members, in times past, fought the battles of British liberties, and frequently lost their lives in the field or resigned them on the scaffold for the sake of maintaining the freedom of their country. Such circumstances deserve the gratitude of a people; though they cannot, if alone, preserve an institution in an age which judges everything by the modern doctrine of utility. Present usefulness is the test by which every man and every thing are judged; and the House of Lords must rest its claim to exist on its present services, and not on its past history.

Different persons will form widely different conclusions on such a subject. It was the hope of Mr. Bagehot that the House of Lords, reinforced by life peers or in some other way, might perform excellent service in revising the statutes which the House of Commons sent up to it. Even Mr. Bagehot, however, admitted that the lords hardly made a serious attempt to discharge the duties which, in his judgment, they were especially qualified to fulfil. Less favourable critics would perhaps contend that the functions of the peers are limited by their prudence; that they revise those measures most carefully on which the public mind is the least excited; and that a hereditary chamber cannot, from its very nature, take any other course.

An institution exactly analogous to the House of Lords cannot be found now, and never existed in the civilised world. The nearest copy to it is perhaps to be traced in the Senate of Canada, whose members are nominated for life by the Governor-General. In the Australian colonies another arrangement has been adopted, and the Legislative Councils are elective, though they are chosen by men of more substance than the electors who choose the representatives for the Houses of Assembly. In Europe, the upper houses of the legislature do not usually consist of hereditary councillors. The Herrenhaus of the Austrian Reichsrath comprises a certain number of hereditary nobles, and a much larger number of life members; the Senate of Italy contains an indefinite number of individuals selected by the Crown, either in consequence of official, literary, or scientific merit, or on account of the amount of taxation which they pay. The Senate in France consists of 300 members, one-fourth of whom hold their positions for life, being appointed to them by the senators themselves; and the remaining three-fourths being elected from time to time by a double process of election by the communes and municipalities. The members of the German Bundesrath are appointed by the governments of the individual states of the Union; and the Senate of the United States consists of two representatives of each state of the Union, appointed by the state legislatures.

Every great country apparently finds it necessary to retain a second chamber. But no great country, except England, makes birth the only or chief qualification for entering it. And a remarkable consequence has ensued from this distinction. In England, where the Upper House owes its existence to birth, the status of individual peers is exceptionally high, but the status of the House of Lords is constantly declining. In the United States and France, where the Senates owe their existence to election, the position of individual senators is comparatively unimportant, but the privileges of the Senate show no symptoms of decline. The Assemblies, which derive their power even indirectly from the people, are thus able to use it; the Assembly, which derives its power from its birth, is continually shrinking from its exercise. It is a logical deduction from this distinction that the country which desires to retain a second chamber should choose an elective and not a hereditary assembly. But mankind is not always governed by logic or submissive to a syllogism ; and it is possible, therefore, that the historic house which has endured for centuries may survive the mushroom chambers of other countries. The hereditary legislators of this country have, in fact, two great advantages. Their rank makes them fortunate in their marriages, their position makes them fortunate in their opportunities. The handsomest, wealthiest, and cleverest girls, by a natural process of selection, marry peers ; and the peerage is recruited by their wealth, their beauty, and their brains. The young nobleman, moreover, finds his opportunity for responsible work at an age when other men are anxiously endeavouring to secure adequate remuneration for the support of themselves or their families. He becomes a responsible member of society at an age when his contemporaries are still regarded as irresponsible boys. Responsibility increases the capacity and enlarges the mind ; and the peer thus inevitably receives, almost before he leaves school, a training which other men do not obtain till their minds have lost the elasticity of youth, and are no longer susceptible to new impressions. These facts probably explain the remarkable position which individual peers still retain. The conclusion of Adam Smith that primogeniture produces only one fool in each family is contradicted every day in the House of Lords. Excluding perhaps two great names, the peers, man for man, are superior in intellect, in eloquence, and in administrative capacity to the members of the House of Commons. Hence arises the singular circumstance that while the House of Commons, to quote the judgment of an acute observer, has more sense than any one in it, the wisest members of the House of Lords are usually regarded as having more wisdom than the House in which they sit. In the House of Commons the majority sometimes forces its leaders into the right path; in the House of Lords the leaders are occasionally unable to persuade their followers from wandering into a wrong one.

CHAPTER III.

THE HOUSE OF COMMONS.

In tracing the development of parliamentary government and the history of the House of Lords in the preceding chapters, frequent mention has necessarily been made of the rise of the Commons to power. We have seen how the Conqueror, after Hastings, converted an assembly of the wise men of the nation into a feudal gathering of his tenants-in-chief; how the lesser barons, unable or unwilling to defray the cost of personal attendance at court, deputed two or three of their number to represent them; how the custom which thus arose received the force of law at Runnymede; how, in the middle of the thirteenth century, the sheriffs were desired to secure the election of proper representatives of the men of the county, instead of simply selecting representatives themselves; how a few years later a single reformer, winning a memorable victory over the Crown, decided on admitting borough representatives to Parliament; and how, before the century was closed in which these great reforms were made, the legislature permanently acquired the elements of which it still consists. Yet the wisest man in the thirteenth century could not have anticipated the results which the reforms of his own time were gradually preparing. In the reign of Edward I. it would have seemed mere folly to have predicted that the time would come when the Crown would still reign but no longer govern; when the vast power of the clergy—the first estate—would be represented in Parliament by an insignificant group of twenty-six prelates in the House of Lords; when the Lords themselves would be only allowed to continue as a separate branch of the legislature on the understanding that they should not oppose the will of the Commons on any question of paramount importance; when the Commons, virtually sovereign, would absorb the powers and even the name of the Parliament, and the borough members would shape the policy of the Lower House. In Saxon times the Witenagemot was practically an assemblage of Magnates. The Concilium of the Norman king was a gathering of his feudal tenantry. The Parliament of the nineteenth century is, in ordinary speech, the House of Commons. When a minister consults Parliament he consults the House of Commons; when the Queen dissolves Parliament she dissolves the House of Commons. A new Parliament is merely a new House of Commons.

In the six centuries, which have elapsed since the original constitution of Parliament, the House of Commons has been the subject of changes which have materially affected its character and its composition. In the reign of Edward I. it is believed to have consisted of 406 members—thirty-seven counties and 166 boroughs each returned two representatives. One hundred years afterwards the House did not probably comprise more than 300 members. In the interval some fifty-three boroughs had either lost or surrendered their privileges of representation. From that time the numbers of the House were slowly increased. In 1536 Monmouth received two members, the Welsh counties one member each; Durham and Cheshire which, as Counties Palatine, had been excused representation, were respectively given members in the reign of Henry VIII. and in the reign of Charles II. Henry VI. added or restored eight boroughs; Edward IV., four; Henry VIII., seventeen; Edward VI., twenty-four; Mary, twelve; Elizabeth, thirty-two; James I., twelve; Charles I., nine; and Charles II., two. No new borough was subsequently created by the personal authority of the Crown; and the House of Commons from the days of Charles II. till the days of Anne comprised eighty members for forty English counties, twelve members for twelve Welsh counties, four members for the two English universities, and 417 members for 216 English and Welsh boroughs. In Anne's reign the union with Scotland added forty-five members; the union with Ireland in 1801 added one hundred members.

Thus the history of the House of Commons from the time of Simon de Montfort to the reign of Victoria is roughly divisible into three periods. During the first of these periods—the fourteenth century—its numbers were gradually contracted; during the next four centuries they were frequently expanded; during the present century they have remained stationary. The numbers decreased during the fourteenth century, because representation was regarded as a burden rather than as a privilege. Few men were rich enough to sustain once a year the cost of a journey to London. Even in counties the electors found it necessary to allow the

E

knights whom they chose wages during their absence from home. The borough members, drawn from a more frugal class of the community, were even more reluctant than the country gentlemen to leave their business. Counties and boroughs were consequently both compelled to pay their representatives during their attendance at Parliament. It is almost certain that the wages which the members thus received date from the very earliest period at which there was a representation at all. They were fixed in the reign of Edward II. at 4*s.* a day for a county, and 2*s.* a day for a borough member. But, though these sums represented the ordinary allowances made to representatives, they must not be supposed to have been invariable. The constituency—if the modern word be admissible—tried to get itself represented as cheaply as possible. In the very reign, in which the wages of members were thus definitely fixed, the county of Derby complained that its knights had received £20 as wages though two men could have been found to do the work for half, or less than half, that sum. In 1427 the townsmen of Cambridge agreed with their members for the discharge of their parliamentary duties on half the ordinary allowance. Local bargains of this character made it tolerably plain that the wages would disappear altogether when the position of a member of Parliament became an honour instead of a burden to him who filled it. But the wages, while they existed, formed a large, perhaps insupportable, charge on some of the communities which paid them. In the Parliament of 1406, the wages of members amounted to nearly £5,500; £6,000 was the whole sum which it granted to the Crown. The constituencies therefore paid almost as much to their members as they granted for the support of the kingdom; and a little borough which succeeded in dispensing with its representation saved itself by this means from perhaps one half of its fiscal burdens. The case of the Parliament of 1406 was no doubt an extreme one, but it forcibly illustrates the burden which representation imposed on the smaller boroughs. In 1463 the produce of a grant of a fifteenth and a tenth—the ordinary supply which was granted to the Crown—was estimated to amount to only £37,000. In the reign of Henry VII. it actually sank to £30,000. If these estimates are at all accurate it seems to follow that the wages of members may not unusually have amounted to one-seventh or one-sixth of the whole sum which Parliament voted.

The cost of representation in mediæval times may perhaps be more strikingly illustrated by another example. In 1352, when the population had been reduced by the Black Death, when labourers were scarce, and the survivors were impoverished by the contraction of business due to the plague, Edward III. summoned only one member instead of two representatives from each constituency. The authorities, it seems, thought that the harvest might be neglected if the full number of members were required to attend the Parliament. It is difficult for a modern student of history to realise the conditions of a period when the housing of a harvest could be arrested or facilitated by the attendance of 200 or 400 provincial gentlemen in London. But the story illustrates the alarm which the diminution of population had caused, and the exhaustion or the poverty of the country at the time. The example of 1352 was followed in 1353. In 1354, however, the king reverted to the ordinary course of requiring the return of two members for each constituency; and, with one exception, this course was invariably pursued till representatives were given to Welsh counties and Welsh boroughs, and these new constituencies, being comparatively remote and sparsely peopled, received only one member each.

The knight of the shire occupied a much higher position than the humble burgess who was returned for his borough. Even in the last hundred years a borough member was not allowed to wear spurs in the House of Commons, the distinction being still reserved for the knights who had been elected by the county. The knights were notable knights, esquires, or gentlemen able to be knights, and not of the degree of yeomen or under. They were chosen in the fourteenth century in the county court by the common assent of the whole county, and the franchise was only limited to forty shilling freeholders in the reign of Henry VI. This great act of disfranchisement—for the man who owned a forty shilling freehold in the days of Henry VI. was in a position of affluence—was due to the tumults made by the great attendance of people of small substance and no value. It continued to regulate the county elections for almost exactly four centuries. In its ultimate results it probably operated on the side of freedom. In the earlier times men of substance were less subservient to the influence either of the Crown or of the aristocracy than their humbler neighbours; and the battle of English liberty was fought by the county freeholders with a spirit which the mass of the community would perhaps have hardly displayed.

The knight of the shire was a man of the county which elected him. The borough member was ordinarily a burgess of the borough which he represented.

But the rule was not followed in the case of the borough as invariably as in the case of the county. When the position of a member of Parliament became a privilege, rich men evaded the law by being admitted to the free burghership of the town. The election in a borough was not conducted on the principle which was uniformly in force in the surrounding county. In some towns the whole of the inhabitants, in others the ratepayers, in others again the governing bodies, chose the representatives. Originally, indeed, the borough franchise was probably wide, and included either the whole of the adult male inhabitants of the borough, or those of them, at any rate, who paid scot and lot, as the local and general taxes were called, or enjoyed the freedom of the community. But it was the policy of the Stuarts to limit the franchise, and the restrictions which were thus introduced were continued by decisions of the House of Commons after the Restoration. In consequence of these decisions, a great variety of franchises existed in different boroughs. "Your honourable house"—to quote a remarkable petition which was presented to the House of Commons in the last decade of the eighteenth century—"is but too well acquainted with the tedious, intricate, and expensive scenes of litigation which have been brought before you in attempting to settle the legal import of the numerous distinctions which perplex and confound the present rights of voting. How many months of your valuable time have been wasted in listening to the wrangling of lawyers upon the various species of burgage-hold, leasehold, and freehold. How many committees have been occupied in investigating the nature of scot and lot, potwallopers, commonalty, populacy, resiant inhabitants, and inhabitants at large. What labour and research have been employed in endeavouring to ascertain the legal claim of boroughmen, aldermen, portmen, selectmen, burgesses, and councilmen; and what confusion has arisen from the complicated operation of clashing charters from freemen, resident and non-resident; and from the different modes of obtaining the freedom of corporations by birth, by servitude, by marriage, by redemption, by election, and by purchase." These complicated and difficult franchises made the work of a returning officer no sinecure. When Romilly stood for Horsham in 1807, only seventy-three electors voted; yet the poll-clerk was occupied for the best part of two days in taking down the description of every burgage tenement from the deeds of the voters. In Weymouth, the right of voting was the title to any portion of certain ancient rents within the borough; and, according to Lord Campbell's autobiography, several electors voted in 1826 as entitled to an undivided twentieth part of sixpence. The returning officer was sometimes occupied a whole day in investigating the title to one of these qualifications. A returning officer naturally required skilled assistance for these investigations, and Lord Campbell, who on one occasion acted as assessor at Cirencester, relates that in the course of the election he decided upon sixty disputed votes, "each of which was like an appeal at Quarter Sessions or a cause at Nisi Prius."

Elections conducted in this extraordinary fashion necessarily occupied a good deal of time. There was no limit to the time for which the poll could be open, and the memorable election for Westminster in 1784 was actually protracted over six weeks. This monstrous example, however, proved too much for the politicians of the eighteenth century. A law was passed which limited every election to fifteen days, and made a repetition of the scandal of 1784 impracticable. It must not, however, be supposed that the elections ordinarily occupied the full time allowed by the statute. In the great majority of cases there was never any contest at all. The members of the House of Commons were mostly returned by decayed towns or little villages, and the inhabitants or electors uniformly supported the nominee of their patron. It was stated in 1793 that 309 out of the 513 members belonging to England and Wales owed their election to the nomination either of the Treasury or of 162 powerful individuals. The 45 Scotch members were nominated by 35 persons. In 1801, 71 out of the 100 Irish members owed their seats to the influence of 55 patrons. The House of Commons, therefore, consisted of 658 members, and of these 425 were returned either on the nomination or on the recommendation of 252 patrons.

Any one who will take the trouble of reflecting on the meaning of these remarkable figures will be in a position to appreciate the leading features of the constitutional history of modern England. From the earliest period to the Revolution of 1688, the main interest in the constitutional history of England consists in the progress of the protracted struggle between the Crown on the one hand and the Parliament on the other. The great issue, which was perpetually at stake through the fifteenth, sixteenth, and seventeenth centuries, was the question whether the country should be governed by King alone, or by King, Lords, and Commons. But the issue which was at stake after the Revolution of 1688 was as momentous. It involved the question whether Parliament should owe its origin to the people at large, or to a small and dwindling oligarchy of powerful borough-owners. It required a civil war to decide the one issue. The other was settled more peaceably by the Reform Act of 1832.

The power of the borough-owners naturally rested on the retention of the representation by small places which had literally no inhabitants, or whose inhabitants were under the irresistible influence of their patron. Some boroughs had almost literally no inhabitants. Gatton was a park; Old Sarum a mound; Corfe Castle a ruin; the remains of what once was Dunwich were under the waves of the North Sea. But the great mass of boroughs were a little more populous than these places, and contained a dozen, fifty, or even one hundred dependent electors. These boroughs, however, insignificant as they mostly were, had originally comprised every place in the country of much importance; and Hallam declared that " if in running our eyes along the map we find any seaport, as Sunderland or Falmouth, or any inland town, as Leeds or Birmingham, which has never enjoyed the elective franchise, we may conclude at once that it has emerged from obscurity since the reign of Henry VIII."

Unequal then as the representation was, its inequalities had been rather the result of accident than of design. Down to the middle of the seventeenth century, every really populous town received representation in Parliament, and the anomaly which arose afterwards of vast centres of industry and wealth without voice in the legislature, had not occurred. From the middle of the seventeenth century, however, the composition of the House of Commons remained unaltered till 1832. The

House, which had previously been modified in every reign, received no new modifications—other than the admission of Scotch and Irish representatives to it—for 160 years. By a strange accident, moreover, parliamentary representation was "stereotyped" at the precise moment when the conditions of social life in England were changed. There were probably 2,300,000 persons living in England and Wales at the close of the reign of Edward III. There were only 5,000,000 or 5,500,000 at the date of the Revolution. But the people, which had taken three centuries to multiply their numbers from 2,300,000 to 5,000,000 or 5,500,000, increased to nearly 14,000,000 in 1831. This increase in the numbers of the people supplied the great irresistible force which ultimately secured the reform of Parliament.

Mere numbers, indeed, only imperfectly explain the nature of the increase which had taken place in the population of the country. In Plantagenet times the people chiefly inhabited the southern counties and the towns which had been erected on southern watersheds. Liverpool was a little group of cottages; Manchester was a village; Birmingham a sand-hill; and the wealth and trade of the country were mainly concentrated in London, Norwich, and Bristol. The industrial revolutions of the eighteenth century, the introduction of steam, the invention of machinery, the construction of roads and canals, altered these conditions. Coal became the first element in the production of wealth, and the population, in consequence, moved to the coal-fields. The northern counties of England, which had hitherto contained large tracts of desolate moorland, became the centres of industry, and great and busy towns were erected in the hitherto remote and solitary valleys of

Lancashire and Yorkshire. The increasing populousness of the northern counties made their representation ludicrously inadequate. In 1831 the ten southern counties of England and Wales comprised a population of 3,260,000 persons, and returned 235 members to Parliament; the six northern counties contained a population of 3,594,000 persons, and returned sixty-six members to Parliament; Lancashire, with 1,330,000 people, had fourteen representatives; Cornwall, with 300,000 inhabitants, had forty-four representatives. In round numbers, every 7,500 persons in Cornwall, and every 100,000 people in Lancashire, had a member to themselves. It required a very fervent faith in the supreme fitness of existing things to induce any one to acquiesce in a disproportion of this character. The great unrepresented towns, like Manchester, Birmingham, and Leeds, were continually inquiring, with a louder and a louder voice, why they should have no share in the government of the country while the owners of a Surrey park, a Wiltshire hill, and a Dorsetshire ruin, had their two members each? The publication of a regular census in 1801, and in every succeeding decade, gave them unimpeachable figures for the support of their arguments. The growing density of population in the north was established by returns which every politician could quote, and to which every reformer could appeal. Representative abuses had been sufficiently glaring before, they became indefensible after the census was once taken.

Parliamentary reform thus became a great political question. The statesmen of the eighteenth century had already admitted its necessity and attempted to deal with it. Chatham, Wilkes, the Duke of Richmond, and William Pitt, all brought forward proposals for the purpose; and a moderate measure, readjusting the political balance, seemed probable. Such a measure might, indeed, have been carried if revolution in France had not been accompanied by excesses which paralysed the arms of reformers and strengthened the forces to which they were opposed. Political progress was summarily arrested by the alarm which French violence produced; and the statesmen by whom this country was governed devoted their whole energies to crushing France, and refused to rectify a single abuse in the government of the British people. The lamentable reaction which arrested progress and stopped reform could be traced in literature as well as in politics, in opinions as well as in laws. But happily for the liberties of England, while the political prospect was shrouded with gloom, a gleam of increasing light shone on British industry. Repressive statutes, unwarranted prosecutions, even a heavy and augmenting taxation, produced no effect on the rising industries which Hargreaves and Arkwright, Crompton and Cartwright, Watt and Boulton, Telford and Brindley, had created by their inventions. These men "had unconsciously been doing the work of the reformers. Manchester had grown from a tiny village to a mighty town; Birmingham was speaking with the voice of a hundred thousand people; Leeds and Sheffield had each fifty thousand inhabitants; Leith, Paisley, and Stockport had twenty thousand each; London, ever extending its limits, had spread far beyond its ancient boundaries; and Marylebone, Finsbury, the Tower Hamlets, Lambeth, and Greenwich were thriving suburbs teeming with humanity. None of these places had any representation. The busy town of Devonport had no member, but the neighbouring villages of Plympton and Saltash had two members each. The fashionable watering-place, Brighton, had no member, but the neighbouring hamlet of Seaford had two members. The short-sighted statesmen of the day thought that these anomalies were productive of the happiest consequences. Nothing, in their view, was so convenient as a nomination borough; nothing was so inconvenient as a contested election in a large constituency."[1] "The first minister of the Crown," said Macaulay, "declared that he would consent to no reform; that he thought our representative system, just as it stood, the masterpiece of human wisdom; that, if he had to make it anew, he would make it just as it was, with all its represented ruins and all its unrepresented cities." Yet there were stronger influences at work than the utterances of statesmen. They were inveighing against all reform, and the steady growth of a new and populous England was, all the while, making reform inevitable.

It is hardly necessary to refer in any detail to the events which preceded the Reform Act of 1832. A solitary Cornish borough was disfranchised, and the two members which it had returned were allotted to Yorkshire; but, with this single exception, nothing was done. Canning deliberately prided himself on opposing the Reformers to the utmost extent of his power; the Duke of Wellington's administration was almost wrecked in 1828 on the miserable question whether, if Retford were disfranchised for bribery, its two members should be given to the hundred in which it was situated

[1] I have ventured to reproduce here a passage from a larger work, *History of England*, vol. ii. p. 265.

or to the great town of Birmingham. While, however, public men in England were thus discussing little technicalities of no real significance, events were preparing in France which were already portending the Revolution of July. Every country in Europe from the Vistula to the Scheldt trembled under the convulsion which drove Charles X. from the throne, and the Tory government of the Duke of Wellington was succeeded in England by the Whig government of Lord Grey. It was inevitable that any ministry, of which Lord Grey was the chief, should endeavour to deal with the great question of reform. The new minister had begun his parliamentary career by advocating the reform of Parliament. Throughout a long career he never altered the principles which he had avowed on his first entrance to public life; he fittingly concluded his political existence by carrying the measure which he had advocated at the commencement of it. It would be impossible in these pages to relate the progress of the struggle which preceded the victory; all that is possible here is to indicate the changes which the great Reform Act made.

The House of Commons comprised 658 members. Up to 1832, 513 of these represented England and Wales, 100 Ireland, and 45 Scotland. In 1832, Ireland received 105 members, Scotland 54; and the remaining 499 members were given to England and Wales. In England 56 boroughs were deprived of their entire representation of 111 members; 31 boroughs were deprived of half their representation; 22 boroughs were given two members each; 24 boroughs one member each; 27 counties were given two additional members; and 7 counties one additional member. Changes so vast would have been thought impossible only a few years before; they were actually received with ridicule when they were first proposed in 1831. They were carried by the enthusiasm of the people out of doors, and their avowed determination to accept the bill, the whole bill, and nothing but the bill. But this vast measure of disfranchisement and enfranchisement was accompanied with another revolution. Up to 1832 the county members had been invariably elected by an uniform constituency—the county freeholders; the borough members had been elected by different kinds of electors in different places. The act of 1832 exactly reversed this condition. The complicated borough franchises were swept away; and, except for the preservation of the rights of freemen and freeholders, the borough franchise was confined to householders whose houses were worth not less than ten pounds a year. The county franchise, on the contrary, was enlarged by the admission of copyholders, of leaseholders, and of tenants whose holding was of the clear annual value of fifty pounds.

This great change constituted the largest revolution which had ever been peaceably effected in any country. Its consequences were, perhaps, only imperfectly visible to the very men who had prepared and accomplished it. Yet one striking fact must have been obvious to any clear thinker. The vast majority of the House of Commons was to be composed of borough members, and the borough members were almost exclusively to be elected by ten pound householders. The majority of the householders necessarily represented the middle classes of the population, and for nearly forty years, therefore, England was practically governed by the middle class.

De Tocqueville remarks, in his famous work on democracy in America, that the government of the middle classes appears to be the most economical, though perhaps not the most enlightened, and certainly not the most generous, of free governments. His observation might receive many illustrations from any careful review of English history from 1832 to 1867. During the whole of this period, however, a demand was continually arising for the extension of the franchise to the lower orders. Reform had been carried in 1832 by the energies of an entire nation, and the masses of the people found, after the struggle was over, that they had only secured the franchise for persons a little better off than themselves. They naturally refused to acquiesce in this result, and from 1832 to 1867 frequently demanded their own enfranchisement. These demands were made with especial vigour in the decade which preceded 1848 and in the decade which preceded 1867. In the first of these periods the people, organised for the purpose, demanded, with arms in their hands, the six points of the Charter. In the latter of them, under the guidance of wiser leaders, they conducted a more peaceable agitation for less violent measures. The close rivalry of the two great political parties in the state facilitated their efforts; and the leader of the Tory party in the Commons, who hated the middle classes and the Whigs much more than he feared the reformers and the people, proved a powerful ally. Furnished by competent advisers with a new Reform Bill, Mr. Disraeli flung away the securities which had made it, on its introduction, tolerable to his own friends, and carried to their amazement a vast measure of reform. The act of 1832 had enfranchised the middle classes; the act of 1867 placed political power in the hands of the lower orders.

By the act of 1867 Ireland retained 105 members, Scotland was allotted 60 members, and England and Wales received 493 members. Of the latter 162 are returned by counties, five by universities, and 326 by boroughs. In England and Wales every freeholder whose freehold is of the annual value of 40s. a year, every copyholder and leaseholder of the annual value of £5, every householder whose rent is not less than £12 a year, is entitled to a vote for the county. Every householder in a borough, and every lodger who pays £10 a year for his lodging, who have been resident for more than twelve months, are entitled to vote for the borough member. In the county the freeholder, and in the borough the lodger, is compelled to make his claim to vote. In the borough any householder, who has before the 20th of July in any year paid the rates due from him up to the previous 5th of January, is entitled to be placed on the register. In Scotland the franchise is not dissimilar from that of England. Owners of land worth £5 a year have a county vote, householders who have paid their poor rates, and lodgers who have paid £10 a year for their lodgings, a borough vote. In Ireland freeholders of £10, copyholders or leaseholders having a sixty years' lease, the value of whose copyhold or leasehold exceeds by at least £10 the rent or charge upon it, have a county vote. Leaseholders, having a twenty years' lease of the clear value of £20, have also a county vote. The borough franchise is confined to householders rated at not less than £4 a year.

In Great Britain, at any rate, the franchise which has thus been fixed for boroughs is so wide that hardly any one is interested in urging its further extension; and the efforts of reformers are directed to securing the assimilation to it of the county franchise, and a further redistribution of political power. In Ireland, on the contrary, reformers naturally complain that the county franchise has not been extended since 1832, and that the borough franchise is less liberal than that which has been applied to England. They are, therefore, unanimous in demanding a further measure of reform. It does not fall within the plan of this volume to discuss the shape which that reform will probably assume. But it requires no great sagacity to predict that every householder, in every part of the kingdom, not disqualified by youth, by crime, by pauperism, or by incapacity, will ultimately receive a vote for a member of Parliament.

Down to 1867 the elector had one vote for every vacancy in the representation of the county or of the borough in which he voted. The elector for the City of London had, for example, four votes, the elector for Westminster two votes, the elector for Aylesbury one vote. Advanced thinkers, however, declared that the system insured only the representation of majorities, and did not give an adequate representation to minorities. Mr. Hare accordingly proposed, and Mr. John Stuart Mill enthusiastically supported, a scheme for the representation of minorities. It may be doubted whether, notwithstanding Mr. Mill's advocacy, the scheme was ever really understood by the mass of Englishmen, or whether it was sufficiently simple for adoption by a practical people. In place of it, in 1867, the legislature allowed each voter in those places which had more than two members one vote less than there were vacancies. The minority in a three-cornered constituency, as it was called, would, it was thought, be always able to return one member out of three. The result has not always coincided with this expectation; and the member representing the minority is also under the disadvantage that he is precluded from accepting office, since his acceptance of it would vacate his seat, and he would in that case have to appeal, not to the minority which elected him, but to the whole of the electors, who certainly would not have elected him. Some future Parliament may devise means for overcoming this difficulty. Till it is overcome the member of the minority is obviously under a serious disqualification.

CHAPTER IV.

PARLIAMENTARY QUALIFICATION AND ELECTORAL CORRUPTION.

IN the earlier stages of national development society wears a simple aspect. The classes of which it is composed are easily defined and easily distinguished. In Saxon times there was a broad distinction between the king and the noble, the noble and the freeman, the freeman and the serf. In Norman times the country was organised on a territorial basis, but the varieties of rank were equally plain. But the artificial distinctions of wealth which were introduced in later periods had no origin in those early ages. When the men of a county or the inhabitants of a borough met together for counsel, no one inquired into the pecuniary qualification of his neighbour. No one presumed to doubt that the voice of the poor man was as good as that of the rich one. Both were equally eligible, provided both were men of full age and free.

Originally in this country there were three qualifications for public business, which could be conveniently described as sex, age, and condition; and two out of the three were uniformly insisted on. No one would have permitted the interference either of woman or serf in public affairs; and neither women nor serf attempted to interfere. But the third qualification was not always attended to. Youths under twenty-one years of age were elected to the House of Commons. They sat there, two centuries and a half ago, as Coke declared, "by connivance." Parliament, indeed, frequently objected to the presence of boys at its deliberations, and at the close of the seventeenth century passed a statute to prevent the election of minors. Little attention, however, had been paid to the old rule that the member should be of age; little obedience was shown to the statute. Almost down to our own times it was occasionally disregarded; and Fox, Liverpool, and Lord John Russell are familiar examples of statesmen who commenced their parliamentary career before they were twenty-one years old.

Down to the close of the fourteenth century, sex, age, and condition formed the only qualifications for a seat in Parliament. The county member, indeed, was expected to be a man of substance—a notable knight, or esquire able to be knight:—and in the reign of Henry VI. a law was passed which required him to have an estate of £600 in land. The law, passed by the same Parliament, which limited the county franchise to freeholders of 40s. a year, was the first instance in this country of wealth, as wealth, being made a qualification for public business. Nearly three centuries passed before a qualification similar to that imposed on the county member was required for the borough member. In the reign of Anne, however, the borough member, like the county member, was compelled to possess a real property qualification. The knight of the shire was still to have his £600 a year in real estate. A property of half this value was deemed adequate for the borough representative.

These qualifications naturally gave a large and ultimately an undue weight to a single interest. A Parliament which could only consist of landlords was not likely to press hardly on the landed classes; and perhaps much of the consideration which the legislature paid to real property was attributable to the qualification thus required of every member of the House of Commons. In this century, however, a qualification based on real estate became too absurd and too unequal to be tolerated. The real property of the kingdom represented only a portion of its wealth; and it became impossible to contend that the man who had placed his money in the funds instead of investing it in land should be disqualified from entering the House of Commons. At the commencement of the present reign the qualification was accordingly altered, and the members were enabled to qualify either in respect of realty or personalty, or both. This alteration, however, did not remove the objection which Radicals naturally entertained to the retention of any qualification whatever. Wealth, in any shape or form, could not, from their point of view, be accepted as a passport to the legislature. The Chartists demanded the abolition of the qualification as one of the six points of the Charter; and, in recent years, it was quietly abandoned. It may, perhaps, be worth while adding that with the exception of the ballot it is the only point of the People's Charter which has yet been carried in its integrity.

It would have been happy for this country if pecuniary means had been made the only qualification for a man's entrance to Parliament. Unhappily, the legislature thought it necessary to add a very different requirement. Towards the end of the seventeenth century a man's faith was made another test of his capacity to serve his country. The ruling classes, alarmed at the evident sympathy of a worthless king with the Church of Rome, and frightened at the stories of Roman Catholic conspiracies which were circulating on every side, decided on excluding the Roman Catholics from Parliament. They did so by compelling every member of the legislature to take certain oaths of allegiance, supremacy, and abjuration which no Roman Catholic could conscientiously take. The oaths proved effectual enough. No Roman Catholic sat in Parliament until after the oaths themselves were altered in 1829; but, as frequently happens on such occasions, the oaths had a much wider effect than had been originally intended. They had been designed to exclude the Papists, and they excluded the Quakers. The Quakers, indeed, did not dissent from any of the statements which the oaths contained, but they conscientiously objected to swear at all. John Archdale, a Quaker whose name still lives in connection with the intolerance which disqualified him, was formally excluded from Parliament on these grounds at the close of the seventeenth century. The Quakers, however, were a peaceful and unambitious sect, and acquiesced in the exclusion; and for 135 years no Quaker was permitted to serve in Parliament. In the interval, however, the legislature had gradually provided for the scruples of these people. Various statutes had been passed for their relief, and an Act of George II. finally enabled them to make an affirmation in all cases in which an oath was required by law. At last, in 1833, Mr. Joseph Pease, the member of a rich and influential family in the north of England, and a Quaker, was elected to sit in the first Reformed Parliament. He claimed to take his seat on making an affirmation, and the House of Commons, on the advice of a Select Committee, admitted the claim. Without tumult, without ostentation, Mr. Pease had won an important victory, and the House of Commons had taken a fresh step in advance.

Four years before Mr. Pease's admission, the election of O'Connell, a Roman Catholic, for an Irish county, had led to the victory known in history as Roman Catholic Emancipation. The legislature, recognising the impossibility of permanently excluding from the House of Commons the chosen representative of a great constituency, consented to repeal the political disabilities of the Roman Catholics. In their case it substituted a new oath for the oath which all members had been previously required to take. From thenceforward all British subjects born in the kingdom or of British parents abroad, of full age and adequate estate, were entitled whatever was their creed to sit in Parliament, provided they had no conscientious objection to an oath and could take the oath of abjuration "on the true faith of a Christian."

Down to 1829 Roman Catholics had been excluded from the legislature by some words in the oath of supremacy which no conscientious Roman Catholic could take. In a similar way Jews were excluded from the legislature by some words in the oath of abjuration. It required an agitation protracted over nearly thirty years to effect the reform which admitted the Roman Catholics. It required an agitation of equal duration to obtain admission to Parliament for the Jews. The bills which after 1832 were introduced for this purpose, and which constantly passed the Commons, were continually rejected by the Lords. Social influences, however, were during the whole period fighting for religious freedom. "The richest man in London was a Jew, the richest man in Paris was the brother of the richest man of London, and Cæsar in Vienna was making Jews barons of the empire." The wealth of the Jews made even Protestants tolerant. In 1828 the City of London agreed to admit baptised Jews to the privileges of citizenship. In 1832 a Jew, for the first time in British history, was called to the Bar; in 1836, a Jew was elected governor of Christ's Hospital; and in 1837, one of the Sheriffs of London was able to remark that his predecessor as well as his successor in office had both been Jews.

These concessions to religious freedom paved the way for further reforms, and liberality was promoted by the conduct of the City of London. In 1828 the county of Clare had made the emancipation of the Roman Catholics a necessity by returning O'Connell to Parliament; in 1847 the City of London sent a Jew, Baron Rothschild, to Parliament. In 1851 the borough of Greenwich, imitating the example of the City, elected another Jew, Alderman Salomons, as its representative. Both members, in taking the oaths, omitted the words " on the true faith of a Christian" from the abjuration oath. Both of them were ordered to withdraw, and, in each case, the House passed resolutions that the member was not entitled to sit and vote. The House, however, did not proceed to declare the seats vacant; and for eleven years one of the members of the City of London was unable to take his seat in Parliament.

The perseverance of the City, however, indicated that

the end must come. At three general elections—in 1847, in 1852, and in 1857—the electors of the City insisted on returning Baron Rothschild to Parliament. On two other occasions, in 1849 and 1857—when he voluntarily resigned his trust into their hands—he was again returned. It was obvious to most persons that the action of the City made the settlement of the question inevitable. In 1858 the Lords saw the necessity of reconsidering their position. A Tory nobleman had the dexterity to suggest that either House might order, in the case of its own member, the omission from the abjuration oath of the words which were offensive to the Jew. The compromise was adopted, and Baron Rothschild at last took his seat. For some sessions the Jews who happened to be elected for Parliament were sworn under this compromise. In 1866, however, the Lords saw the folly of defending any further a position which had ceased to be of any practical utility. A new oath, applicable to all members, was substituted for the oaths previously in force; and the offensive distinction between Jew and Christian was finally removed.

Any legislator might have been justified in hoping that the adoption of this oath had definitely disposed of the religious difficulty in Parliament. An oath which was so wide that it could be taken without hesitation by Protestant, Roman Catholic, or Jew, an oath for which an affirmation could be substituted by those who had conscientious objections to be sworn, seemed to cover every condition which could possibly arise. In 1880, however, the legislature was suddenly confronted with a new dilemma. The borough of Northampton sent a representative to Parliament who refused to take an oath—not because he had any conscientious objection to be sworn, but because an appeal to a God—in whom he had no belief—seemed to him an idle formula which was not binding on his conscience. This contention lighted up a new controversy. On the one hand, the law had made no provision for the affirmation of a confessed atheist. On the other hand, it was contended that a person to whom an oath had no meaning could not be allowed to take an oath. It was finally decided that the member who had caused the controversy should make an affirmation at his own peril; and that it should be open to any individual to test its sufficiency by an action in the ordinary courts. But this decision only temporarily disposed of the difficulty. The courts held that the House of Commons had no power to substitute an affirmation for an oath; and that the member who had made the affirmation was liable to penalties for sitting without taking the oath. He vacated his seat, and his constituents re-elected him. He claimed a right to be sworn, and the House again refused to allow an oath to be administered to him. No expedient has yet been found for terminating this new dilemma.

Property and creed were the chief qualifications required of members of Parliament. But, in addition to these, the legislature for nearly two centuries has found it necessary to secure the independence of its members by excluding placemen and pensioners from the House of Commons. The earliest attempt to exclude placemen took place in the reign of William III. But the Act of Settlement formally decided that no person who had an office or place of profit under the king, or received a pension from the Crown, should be capable of serving as a member of the House of Commons. Experience, however, soon proved that this famous article was much too wide. Parliament cannot ensure the submission of the executive to its own authority, unless the principal members of the government are personally answerable to it. A rule which excluded the members of the Cabinet from the House of Commons deprived the House of the power of controlling the ministry. Accordingly in 1706 the principle was modified. Members accepting office were directed to vacate their seats; members accepting offices, created subsequently to 1705, were declared incapable of re-election. This rule has been practically maintained till the present time, though the number of offices which entitle their possessors to a seat in Parliament has been slightly enlarged; and the member of a government who exchanges one office for another is not required to be re-elected. As the Crown no longer possesses an indefinite power of creating pensioners, the provision against their admission has been superseded; and the superannuated officials of the state, who owe their pensions to the bounty not of the Crown but of the legislature, are no longer excluded from the House of Commons.

The provisions of the Act of Settlement, excluding placemen and pensioners, only imposed slight difficulties on corrupt ministers in a corrupt age. Men received pensions on the Civil List and pensions from secret service money without the knowledge of Parliament; and the provisions of the Act of 1706, which had enabled the members of a ministry to sit in the House of Commons, had also preserved a crowd of subordinate officials whose places had existed before that year. This abuse was partly remedied in 1743, when an act was passed disabling a large number of placeholders from sitting. Even this act, however, did not terminate the prevalent corruption. In the period of bad government, which immediately succeeded the accession of George III., every attempt was made to influence the House of Commons. In the beginning of the reign two votes for one division were purchased with two peerages; contracts were constantly given for corrupt reasons to members of Parliament; and the House found it necessary to determine that contractors should thenceforward be excluded from sitting in the House of Commons.

So far then as members of the House of Commons are concerned, two influences, based on opposite reasons and tending to contrary results, have been at work during the last two centuries: on the one hand, the barriers, which had been erected to exclude poor men and men who did not profess the Protestant faith from the House of Commons, have been gradually broken down; on the other hand, fresh obstacles have been erected to exclude placemen, pensioners, and contractors dependent on the bounty of the Crown or on the favour of the minister. In the preceding chapter an account has already been given of the manner in which the electoral franchise has been from time to time altered. The same reign, it may be added, which imposed a property qualification on county members, imposed a property qualification on the county elector. The same causes which drove the Roman Catholic from the House, deprived him of his franchise; and the same measure which restored him to his seat in Parliament, provided him again with a vote. The property qualification of members was abolished only nine years before the borough franchise was extended to every householder. It is obvious, therefore, that legislation, in the case both of elector and member, has proceeded on parallel lines, and that it has been inspired in both cases by the same influences.

One important exception, however, must be made to this rule. In 1782 the contractor was excluded from Parliament; and for the same reason and at the same time the revenue officer was disfranchised. During the last few years the revenue officer has been given back his vote, but the contractor is still disqualified from sitting in the House of Commons. It can hardly be necessary to offer any further explanation of the causes which deprived the contractor of his seat. But a hasty observer may perhaps hardly realise the difference which made the disfranchisement of revenue officers a necessity in 1782, and which deprived their enfranchisement of all significance in our own time. Ten years after 1782, a majority of the whole House of Commons was returned by constituencies none of which had two hundred and fifty, and in the great majority of which there were not one hundred, voters. A dozen revenue officers could obviously exercise a great, perhaps a decisive, influence in an election confined to 50, 100, and even 200 persons; and, in one Cornish borough, in which eleven persons were entitled to vote, ten out of the eleven are said to have been revenue officers of the Crown. The efforts of Burke, and the determination of the Rockingham ministry to disfranchise a few subordinate officials, receive a new light from the circumstances of this borough.

The disfranchisement of these officers at the close of the eighteenth century was, in fact, a welcome proof that Parliament was at last obtaining superiority in its long struggle with the Crown. Their enfranchisement in the last half of the nineteenth century showed that the constitution had been founded on too broad a basis to make the future interference of the Crown a probable or even possible danger. One form of corruption had been effectually prevented. Parliamentary corruption, however, had not been terminated; it had merely taken a new shape. The House of Commons had not been purified; it had only changed the manner of its offending. In the eighteenth century its members had received bribes; in the nineteenth century they gave bribes. In the eighteenth century its members were seduced; in the nineteenth century they practised the art of seduction. Society deals with political seduction much as it deals with seduction in private life. It ostracises the victim, and pardons the seducer. It smiles on the briber, and denounces the bribed.

Parliamentary corruption is usually supposed to be a weed of modern growth, fostered in the last century, and propagated with amazing activity after the Reform Act of 1832; and, in the modern sense in which the term is used, this conclusion is sufficiently accurate. The great majority of the electors before 1832 were not bribed, for the simple reason that it was unnecessary to bribe them. Lord Monson's butler at Gatton, the Duke of Newcastle's tenants at Newark, the revenue officers at Harwich, voted as their masters desired them; the little unreformed constituencies were pure because they were too dependent to be corrupt. Corruption, however, at least as debasing as that with which modern England is infected, may be traced in the earliest periods of English history. But as the supreme power has gradually passed from a king to an oligarchy, and from an oligarchy to a people, so the bribes which used to be given to king and oligarchs are now paid to the mass of the electors. When the king was supreme, ambitious men bribed him to give them place; and the sale of offices became a regular source of income. When the borough owners became supreme, they sold their boroughs or their votes; and their purchase was a regular expedient for conducting the government. When the people became supreme, bribery, in its modern shape, was used to influence hundreds and even thousands of electors. And so people were startled by the growth of corruption. Yet corruption was not increased; it was merely diffused.

The history of parliamentary corruption may, in this way, be said to reflect the gradual passage of power from the king to an oligarchy, from an oligarchy to a people. In the old days, however, no one would have thought of purchasing a seat in Parliament, because parliamentary attendance was regarded as a burden instead of a privilege; and boroughs and counties, instead of selling their seats, were compelled to pay their representatives wages. It became a fashion in Tudor times for rich men to come to London; the attractions of Elizabeth's court allured them to the metropolis as moths and flies are allured to the candle. Instead of being a burden, a seat in Parliament became a privilege, and the gentlemen who aspired to it, instead of expecting wages, were ready to pay for the distinction. The payment of members was gradually discontinued, and the bribery of electors began. In 1571 Thomas Long gave the Mayor of Westbury the sum of £4 to ensure his return. It is obvious that, according to Long's notions, a seat in Parliament even in 1571 was worth £4. The rapid development of wealth in the seventeenth and eighteenth centuries increased the price of the seats in a very striking manner. At the beginning of the reign of George III. Selwyn received £9,000 for the two seats at Ludgershall; and throughout the reign £10,000 was probably procurable, wherever parties were evenly balanced, for the two seats of a borough.

This scandalous traffic in seats continued unchecked till 1809. In that year an act was passed declaring the sale of seats to be illegal. But the act proved a very imperfect remedy for the evil which had arisen. It did not apply to the sale of burgage tenures; it did not prohibit the promise of office in return for a vote. It therefore placed no restraint on the influence of the government, and hardly any restraint on the action of individuals.

It must not be supposed, indeed, that all the borough owners sold their seats. Most of them, on the contrary, retained them in their own hands for the sake of advancing their immediate interests, or of obliging their political friends. A man who owned a borough could usually command a peerage or an embassy for himself, a pension for his wife, or an appointment for his son, by placing one of the seats at the disposal of the minister. The art of government was almost synonymous with the art of corruption, and men were placed in situations because they possessed parliamentary influence; while highly-paid situations were maintained for the sake of purchasing—legally purchasing—the assistance of the borough owners.

There were, indeed, throughout the whole period a

few boroughs whose representatives were chosen on a different system, and whose election did not depend on the nomination of a single individual. But these boroughs were usually as corrupt as the great noblemen and commoners who sold their influence for peerages or money. Lord John Russell stated in the House of Commons in 1831 that men were openly paid for their votes at Liverpool. "By long-established custom," wrote Wilberforce, "the single vote of a resident elector at Hull was rewarded with a donation of two guineas; four were paid for a plumper, and the expenses of a freeman's journey from London averaged £10 a-piece. The letter of the law was not broken, because the money was not paid till the last day on which election petitions could be presented." Lord Campbell's authority may be quoted for the existence of a similar system at Stafford; £7 was given for a single vote, £14 for a plumper, to be paid about a twelvemonth after the election. Lord Cochrane, after his return for Honiton, sent the town-crier round the borough to tell the voters to go to the chief banker for £10 10*s.* each. The Corporation Commissioners of 1835 reported that, in 1826, the borough of Leicester had spent £10,000 of the borough funds in securing the election of a political partisan. Bribery was accompanied by riot and treating. A contested election in a popular constituency involved a fortnight of riot and drunkenness. "This," wrote Buxton at Weymouth during the General Election of 1826, "is the sixth day of polling, and there is every probability of six days more. The election is carried on with the utmost violence and at monstrous expense. It is said that —— spends £1,500 a day, and his party confesses to £1,000. He has nine public-houses open, where any body, male or female, is very welcome to eat and get drunk; and the truth is, the whole town is drunk."

These scandalous proceedings were undoubtedly encouraged by the attitude of the House of Commons. Nominally every one in Parliament reproved them; in reality every one laughed at them. Before the reign of George III. an election could only be reversed by the House itself; it could only be reversed afterwards by a select committee of the House; and the House and its committees were more anxious to settle the question on political grounds than to punish corruption. We, who in the nineteenth century are astounded at the pertinacity with which the Commons clung to the privilege of determining their own elections, are perhaps apt to lay inadequate stress on the circumstances on which the claim was originally made. Up to 1406 the sheriff had returned the writ in full Parliament, and the king had taken cognisance of complaints respecting the validity of the election. In 1410 the Judges of Assize were authorised to inquire into undue returns, and, as the judges were appointed by the king and removable at his pleasure, the validity of the election was practically determined by officers under the control of the Crown. In 1586 the Commons displayed their growing independence by asserting their claim to determine the issue themselves. This claim was repeated in the reign of James I., and its assertion was one of the many means by which the House secured its freedom from control. The claim, however, lost all meaning under the House of Hanover. The Crown had neither the power nor the will to control the returning officers, and the contest which in the previous century had lain between the

King and Commons, had degenerated into a struggle between Whigs and Tories. The votes of both parties were directed to secure the predominance of their own friends, and one great minister was actually driven from office by an adverse vote on an election petition.

This system continued in force till 1770. In that year Mr. George Grenville persuaded the members of the House of Commons to intrust the trials of election petitions to committees, instead of conducting them themselves. The committees which were thus chosen were in the first instance selected by ballot. Either party to the petition had the right of rejecting a certain number of the names which were successful in the ballot, and the residue were intrusted with the task of trying the election. It was obvious that the committees thus instituted were only slightly less prejudiced than the House itself. The House had decided the issue on party grounds, the committee decided it according to the political opinions of the majority. The old system had produced a party struggle on the petition itself; the new system resulted in a party struggle on the ballot for the committee.

The scandals which have been indicated in this chapter continued unremedied until 1832. In 1832 the legislature limited the duration of elections to two days, and thus stopped for ever the protracted disturbances which these struggles had previously produced. Seven years afterwards, or in 1839, the House of Commons decided on intrusting the selection of election committees to a general committee of selection. In 1844 the committees which were thus formed were limited to five members; and in the last few years a further step has been taken, and the trial of election petitions has been referred to a judge; or, later still, to two judges of the High Court of Justice.

It was hoped that a less partial tribunal than an election committee would discourage corruption. Bribery, however, was not the only evil which a reformed legislature had to deal with. Experience showed that, while some electors were paid for their votes, others were intimidated into voting with their employers or their landlords. Intimidation, like bribery, existed in an unreformed Parliament; and the Duke of Newcastle's speech, on ejecting his tenants at Newark who had voted against his candidate, was one of the many causes which promoted the passage of the first Reform Act. But intimidation, like bribery, became a much more prevalent evil when the number of electors was multiplied and the franchise was extended to a more dependent class of persons; and a cry was consequently raised for protection for the voter. The ballot was originally recommended by the ministerial committee which drew up the first Reform Act. It was annually advocated by Mr. Grote, the historian of Greece, in the House of Commons. It constituted one of the six demands which the Chartists embodied in their Charter, and it was afterwards continually recommended by other advocates. But for thirty-five years the question made no progress. The franchise—it was declared—was a trust. The elector—like his representative—was bound to discharge his trust in public; and the same reasons, therefore, which had led to the publication of debates and division lists in Parliament, militated against the adoption of secret voting in the constituencies. Till after the general election of 1868, nothing seemed so unlikely as the adoption of the ballot. The experience, however, of a single year converted a nation. The electors, drawn under the Act of 1867 from the most dependent classes of the community, obviously required protection. The inconveniences, resulting from the adoption of the ballot, were discovered to be smaller than those which were inseparable from its refusal ; and Parliament was persuaded to institute the experiment, and substitute secret for open voting.

Intimidation has been checked to some extent by the adoption of the ballot; but corruption has not been materially diminished by its use. Bribery still flourishes, though the briber is unable to test decisively the result of his bribe ; and the example of the general election of 1880 has proved that many small and some comparatively large towns are still corrupt. Yarmouth, Chester, Oxford, Gloucester, and Macclesfield, are examples of important towns where corruption has been prevalent ; and bribery, like drunkenness, will apparently continue till society sees that it is a disgrace to be corrupt, and a disgrace to be drunk. So long as men in high positions feel themselves in honour bound to pay bills which they know to be illegal, and which it ought therefore to be dishonourable to pay ; so long as men of rank associate with men whom they know to be guilty of corruption ; so long as commissioners appointed to investigate corrupt practices laugh at the abuses which they ought to reprove, there is little hope of terminating bribery. The best hope of terminating it is to be found neither in the ballot, nor in penal laws, but in the gradual growth of healthier manners.

CHAPTER V.

PREROGATIVE AND PRIVILEGE.

THE student of constitutional history who examines the relations between the Crown and the Parliament continually meets with two words—prerogative and privilege. In modern history, at any rate, he finds the former universally applied to the power inherent in the Crown, the latter with few exceptions used to express the rights of the legislature. Yet, if the historical student will turn from his Stubbs, his Hallam, or his May, to any dictionary, he will find that the words, notwithstanding the distinctive sense which they have acquired, were originally interchangeable. Privilege, says Johnson, is a peculiar advantage; prerogative is an exclusive or peculiar privilege.

The relations of the Crown with the legislature are very simple. The Crown summons Parliament; it prorogues Parliament; it dissolves Parliament. In the earlier times the Crown was compelled to summon Parliament "once a year, or more often if need be." Since the reign of Charles II. it has been bound to issue writs for the summoning of a new Parliament within three years after the determination of an old one. These laws, however, are practically obsolete. For nearly two centuries the legislature has effectually provided for its own convention by making government without its assistance impracticable. If a Parliament were not convened, the army would be disbanded and the machinery of government would stand still with the stoppage of the annual supplies. In theory, however, the Crown has the right to decide when a Parliament shall meet; it is also its prerogative to appoint the place at which it shall be held. The new Parliament is always opened by a speech delivered either by the Crown itself or by commissioners appointed by the Crown, detailing the measures which Parliament has been summoned to consider. Parliament, however, is not bound to confine its attention to those matters which have been thus commended to its consideration by the Crown; and, by one of those curious customs which are relics of an age when the contest between Crown and legislature was sharp, both Houses are accustomed to mark their independence by reading for a first time some bill of their own before they take the Crown's message into consideration.

The Crown, which has the right to summon a Parliament, has also the right to determine its session or its existence. In the former case it prorogues, in the latter it dissolves, the Parliament. Prorogation and dissolution have both the effect of terminating all the business which Parliament is transacting. In a new session every matter has to be recommenced anew; and, as a bill which has been rejected once cannot be re-introduced in the same session, Parliament has occasionally been prorogued for a short interval to allow its speedy re-introduction in a new session. When Parliament is actually sitting, it is usually prorogued by some high official speaking in the presence of the sovereign, or by her authority. In practice a Parliament is never prorogued for more than eighty days; at the expiration of this period, however, it can be prorogued for any further time by proclamation. Even in those cases, in which the dissolution of a Parliament has been determined upon, it has been the almost uniform practice in the first instance to prorogue it. Charles II., however, personally dissolved Parliament in 1681. The Prince Regent personally dissolved Parliament in 1818. Of recent years the usual course has been to announce the impending dissolution in the prorogation speech; and to issue the proclamation dissolving the legislature immediately afterwards.

When a Parliament is dissolved the Crown is compelled to give thirty-five days notice of the time of holding a new one. When Parliament is only prorogued, the Crown is compelled to give fourteen days notice of a new session. These arrangements are both comparatively modern. Rapid communication has, in fact, made longer notice unnecessary; and a fortnight, for all practical purposes, is a much longer notice now than six weeks proved before the invention of telegraphs and steam. When a new Parliament meets, an interval necessarily elapses before formal business commences. During the interval the Commons are authorised to elect a Speaker; and both Houses are occupied with the preliminary task of swearing in their members. When this prefatory work is completed, the Commons are summoned to the Lords to hear the speech from the throne, and the work of the Parliament begins. When, on the contrary, an old Parliament meets for a new session, the speech from the throne is at once delivered, and business commenced.

This account of the relations of the Crown with the legislature in summoning, proroguing, and dissolving Parliament applies to the ordinary circumstances of every year. It ought, however, to be added that, on the occasion of the Crown's demise, Parliament at once meets without summons; and that during the incapacity of George III. in 1789 and 1810, Parliament met without the King's personal authority, and was opened by a commission to which the great seal had been attached by the Chancellor. These, however, were temporary expedients adopted in particular conjunctures, and are only accidental exceptions to the operation of the ordinary rule which has been previously described. When the House of Lords is sitting, the Lord Chancellor is *ex officio* Speaker. The Commons, it has already been stated, are instructed by the Crown, at the commencement of every Parliament, to elect a Speaker for Her Majesty's approbation. The highest functionary in the House of Lords is therefore an officer who owes his appointment to the Crown. The highest officer in the House of Commons is chosen subject to the approbation of the Crown. The Crown's approval has, indeed, been long a meaningless form, but it illustrates the usages of another age, when the Crown frequently endeavoured to control the proceedings of the legislature.

In the Lords the Speaker has only a nominal authority. In the Commons he has large powers of enforcing order. His name, indeed, does not convey a clear idea of his functions. In the Commons the Speaker does everything but speak. He is, in fact, the spokesman rather than the speaker of the House; and the first of these high functionaries, Peter de la Mare, who held the office in 1376, was accurately styled the Prolocutor of the Commons. The Speaker acts as spokesman of the Commons at the commencement of every Parliament. He communicates to the Royal Commissioners the Commons' choice of himself, and submits himself "with all humility to Her Majesty's gracious approbation." The Chancellor, as one of the commissioners, addresses him by name, and conveys to him the Crown's approval of his election. As a matter of fact, more than two hundred years have passed since the Crown has ventured to withhold its royal approbation. The Speaker, his election approved, lays claim, on behalf of the Commons of the United Kingdom, to all their ancient and undoubted rights and privileges; and the Chancellor, addressing him as Speaker, is commanded to inform him that Her Majesty does most readily confirm all the rights and privileges which have ever been granted to or conferred upon the Commons by any of her royal predecessors.

The rights and privileges to which the Commons thus lay claim are enjoyed by the Lords as hereditary counsellors of the Crown. The privileges which the Speaker demands for the Commons are particularly freedom of speech in debate; freedom from arrest of their persons and servants; free access to Her Majesty when occasion shall require; and the placing the most favourable construction upon all their proceedings. This claim has been repeated almost in the same words for nearly four centuries. Some of the privileges which are thus demanded have lost their significance; others of them have been secured to the Commons by firmer expedients than the ready approval of the Crown; but the old formula, eloquent of the past, is still repeated at the commencement of every Parliament, and the Commons still profess to ask the Crown in all humility to confer upon them the privileges which their own virtual supremacy makes it impossible for any sovereign to refuse.

It will be seen that the rights and privileges which are thus nominally claimed are divisible into four heads. The right of free access to the throne, is enjoyed by both Houses. But, while the Lords are individually entitled to have access to the sovereign, the Commons only enjoy the right as a body. A right of this kind from its very nature is of little significance. The House, even when it agrees on addresses to the throne, is accustomed to direct the privy counsellors who have seats in it to deliver them; and probably many members of the House of Commons are ignorant that they are entitled as a body to force themselves into their sovereign's presence without putting on a court suit, and that on these occasions they may drive, according to Sir E. May, "through the central mall in St. James's Park," or, in better English, along the central road in the Mall. At the present time, the construction which the Crown is pleased to place upon the proceedings of the House of Commons is almost as immaterial as the privilege of free access to the throne. Members of Parliament in these days think a good deal of what the electors are saying of them; but, with few exceptions, they do not trouble themselves to ascertain the views of the sovereign. It is notorious that both George IV. and William IV. occasionally looked with very little favour on the proceedings of the House of Commons; and that the House forced Catholic Emancipation on the first of these sovereigns, and a Whig ministry on the last of them. But in mediæval England the privilege which was thus claimed and which is still asserted was pregnant with significance. Peter de la Mare, Prolocutor of the Good Parliament in 1376, was arrested; one Haxey was thrown into prison by Richard II. for introducing a proposal which reflected on the Court; Thomas Thorpe, Speaker in 1453, was arrested by the Duke of York, and the Commons failed to procure his release; and one Yonge, who had proposed in 1451 that the Duke of York should be declared heir to the throne, was also arrested. These arrests gave the Commons a vivid interest in claiming a favourable construction for their proceedings. Yet even the concession of this privilege did not secure them. So unfavourable was the construction which Charles I. placed on the proceedings of the Parliament which voted the Petition of Right, that immediately after its dissolution he flung its most eminent members into the Tower and the King's Bench. So unfavourable was the construction which the same monarch placed on the proceedings of the Parliament which framed the Grand Remonstrance, that he endeavoured to seize its five most prominent members within the walls of the House of Commons.

In all the examples quoted in the preceding paragraph, interference with the Commons was attempted by the arrest of the Prolocutor, the Speaker, or some prominent members of the House. It may perhaps be thought that the privilege of freedom of arrest, which is regularly claimed, would have saved the Commons from this danger. This privilege, however, was always limited to civil causes. The Crown, so it was thought, had the first right to the time of every member sent to its council, and no private question was allowed to interfere with this primary duty.

Antiquarians have traced the privileges which members of Parliament thus obtained to the earliest days of English history. "If the king call his people to him and any one does an injury to one of them, let him pay a fine," so ran the old Anglo-Saxon law. The security was given to the counsellor on his road to and from the Witenagemot for a definite number of days before and after its assembly. In mediæval times the privilege which was thus acquired assumed a definite form. As a man could hardly travel through mediæval England without a servant, the member's privilege was extended to his servant. Member and servant were, on the same principle, exempted from arrest for debt, their goods were protected from distress, and, by a perhaps logical extension of the privilege, they were protected from civil actions and from the ordinary liability of other citizens to act as jurors.

The singular privileges which were thus acquired have left their mark on the history of England; and men like Chedder—a member's servant assaulted on his road to the House—or Ferrers—a member whose release from arrest was demanded and obtained in 1543—are still recollected by historical students, because they are associated with the growth and progress of this privilege. So true is it that the heroes of obscure broils, or the defendants in obscure actions, may occasionally be remembered when their greater and better contemporaries are forgotten. During the whole period, when the struggle between Crown and Parliament was keen, the Commons clung to the position which they had gained in the fourteenth and fifteenth centuries. The Revolution, however, which made them supreme, enabled them to surrender some portions of their claims. In 1700 the goods of privileged persons were made liable to distress when Parliament was either dissolved, prorogued, or even adjourned for above a fortnight; and seventy years afterwards the exemption from arrest, which had been previously enjoyed by member's servants, was abandoned. From thenceforward the member was free from arrest in civil actions, but his goods were liable to distress, and the person of his servant was no longer inviolable.

Limited as the privilege was by the changes introduced by the act of 1770, it occasionally became a matter of scandal. Ordinary men in debt could be arrested on mesne process; and the debtor who had powerful friends could avoid his liabilities by obtaining a seat in Parliament. When seats were purchaseable like tickets for the opera, some unscrupulous persons naturally thought that the House of Commons was the best haven for an insolvent; and Lord Beaconsfield described one of the characters in his earliest novel as "so involved that the only way to keep him out of the House of Correction was to get him into the House of Commons." Lord Beaconsfield's sneer was justified by the facts. A few years before he wrote *Vivian Grey* a debtor, a prisoner in the Fleet, had been elected for Beverley. The House of Commons had insisted on his discharge from prison, when, instead of repairing to his parliamentary duties, he departed from the country. The privilege which had been a necessity in one age had become a scandal in another.

Theoretically, the scandal which occurred in the election of a debtor for Beverley sixty years since might recur to-day. But virtually its recurrence is impossible from the course which legislation has assumed. In the first place imprisonment for debt is abandoned; and, in the next place, the disfranchisement of little boroughs and the extension of the franchise, has made entrance to parliamentary life something more than a mere matter of influence. Members of the House of Commons are still free from arrest during the session of Parliament and for a reasonable time before its commencement and after its termination. But no inconvenience has of late years resulted, or is likely to result, from the perpetuation of this privilege.

Three of the great privileges which the Speaker claims at the commencement of every Parliament have been thus briefly dealt with. The fourth requires longer treatment. Freedom of speech, in the ordinary meaning of language, is a very simple proposition. But free speech is attended with such considerable results that it has been liable to certain restraints in every stage of society. Allowed in this country to perhaps the fullest possible extent, it has been followed by other consequences which seem now inseparable from the very existence of a legislature. Free speech has in its turn led to the publication of Parliamentary Reports, to the publication of Parliamentary Division Lists, and to the publication of Parliamentary Papers.

Free speech, an essential condition for a deliberative assembly, was claimed as a parliamentary privilege from the earliest periods. In the reign of Henry VIII. the judges, on a particular complaint, told the king that freedom of speech concerning the matter there debated was no more than what Parliament men ought to have. Their dictum, however, did not settle the question. Towards the close of the century Coke, as Lord Keeper, told the Commons, in reply to their customary claim for privileges, "Liberty of speech is granted you, but you must know what privilege you have, not to speak every one what he listeth or what cometh in his brain to utter; but your privilege is aye or no." And more than thirty years afterwards the greatest of the Eliots died in the Tower, a prisoner for words uttered in his place in Parliament. Happily, however, the proceedings of which Eliot was the victim were formally reversed at a later period. Free speech was again declared to be one of the ancient and necessary rights or privileges of Parliament; and finally, by the Bill of Rights, it was formally declared that the freedom of speech and debates or proceedings in Parliament ought not to be impeached or questioned in any court or place out of Parliament.

In the present age freedom to report words uttered in Parliament has been almost insensibly connected with freedom of speech. An Englishman, surrounded by modern circumstances, can hardly separate the free speech uttered in the House one evening from the report of it which he reads in the newspaper the following morning. But, in former ages, parliamentary reporting was discouraged because it was supposed to interfere with liberty of debate. The members of the House of Commons, in the reign of the second Stuart, were chiefly anxious to conceal their proceedings from the unhappy monarch, who from his faults seemed a despot to his subjects, and who, from his misfortunes, has been crowned martyr by their descendants. The Long

Parliament expressly forbade any member to publish his speech. The old reasons for this decision disappeared with the fall of the monarchy. But the House of Commons, which had destroyed an autocrat, was slowly developing during the next century and a half into a despotic oligarchy. In the seventeenth century it had found convenience in screening its proceedings from the Crown; in the eighteenth century it persisted in screening them from the people. As early as 1694 it resolved that "no news-letter writers do, in their letters or other papers that they disperse, presume to intermeddle with the debates or any other proceedings of this House." The resolution, however, proved only partially effective. The circulation of the news-letters increased; the desire of their readers for authentic news was encouraged; and it proved necessary for the House in 1728 to repeat its resolution and to threaten to proceed with the utmost severity against offenders. The inaccurate reports, indeed, which had appeared in some of the news-letters almost excused the resolutions of the House. "I have read some of the debates of this House, sir," said a great minister in 1738, "in which I have been made to speak the very reverse of what I meant. I have read others of them wherein all the wit, learning, and argument have been thrown into one side, and, on the other, nothing but what was low, mean, and ridiculous; and yet, when it comes to the question, the division has gone against the side which, upon the face of the debate, had reason and justice to support it. So that had I been a stranger to the proceedings and to the nature of the arguments, I must have thought this to have been one of the most contemptible assemblies on the face of the earth." The modern minister, who relies on the press to circulate among millions the arguments which he addresses to hundreds, can perhaps hardly appreciate the feelings of his predecessor who, in another century, saw his reasoning distorted by the imperfect reports of the old news-letters.

The determination of the House to suppress the publication of debates led to curious expedients for evading the decision. *The London Magazine* published "The Proceedings of the Political Club;" *The St. James' Chronicle,* "The Debates of the Representatives of Utopia;" *The Gentleman's Magazine,* "The Debates of the Senate of Lilliput." But the House of Commons naturally resented the transparent subterfuges by which its regulations were evaded. In the bad period of personal government which followed the accession of George III., one more serious attempt was made to punish the publication of debates. Colonel Onslow, a Tory member, seriously proposed to bring the printer and publisher of every reporting newspaper to the bar. His proposal led to one of the most memorable sittings which the House of Commons has ever known. Throughout the whole of a long night the Opposition, led by Burke, resisted the proposal. The minority withstood the decision of the majority in twenty-three divisions; and the majority, though it succeeded in its immediate objects, learned a lesson which it never forgot. The price at which it was possible to obtain the punishment of reporting newspapers was a little too heavy for even the Onslows of the eighteenth century to pay; and members of Parliament gradually abstained from taking formal notice of the publication of their proceedings.

When the publication of debates was once allowed, immense improvements were introduced into the reports. Men like Mr. Woodfall, endowed with prodigious powers of memory, were superseded by practised shorthand writers, capable of placing on their notes every word which was uttered by the most voluble speaker. It was soon perceived that the influence of Parliament was increased a hundredfold by the assistance of the reporters; and, instead of jealously excluding short-hand writers, both Houses made special arrangements for their accommodation. The Lords, who happened to have the necessary space at their disposal, made this concession as early as 1831. The Commons, more cramped for room, were unable to make it till the old and inconvenient chapel, which had been their home for centuries, was destroyed by fire. Long, indeed, after the introduction of shorthand writers the presence of strangers at debates was regarded as a breach of privilege; and any member was able, by drawing the Speaker's attention to their presence, to effect their exclusion. This power, however, could obviously only exist so long as the good sense of all the members prevented its exercise. It was utterly impossible for any deliberative assembly to allow one of its members to decide whether its debates should be reported or not. In the last few years the House has accordingly modified its previous practice. A single member may still draw attention to the presence of strangers, but strangers are not excluded unless the House itself so determine.

Publicity has increased to an extraordinary degree the influence of the House of Commons. Every member who makes a speech in Parliament is aware that the substance, if not the context, of his arguments, may be procured the following day in any part of the United Kingdom for a penny. But publicity has also increased the power of the electors. Every voter has the opportunity of judging how his representative discharges his duty. Many members, indeed, do not speak; but every member has a vote. The publication of debates has naturally led to the publication of division lists; and the use which every gentleman makes of his presence in Parliament is consequently known in the most remote village. Perhaps there are few people who are aware that authoritative lists of divisions have only appeared during the last fifty years; and that even a reformed House of Commons, in its first session, positively refused to take steps for their publication. Accurate lists of each division have been published under the authority of the House of Commons since 1836.

Almost at the very time at which division lists were first published, the House of Commons adopted another liberal measure and sanctioned the sale of its papers. Up to that time these documents had—it was supposed—been printed for the enlightenment of the legislature alone, and the public who were unacquainted with members of Parliament had no means of obtaining access to them. The growing influence of the press, however, made this state of things more and more impossible. It was certain that, in some way or other, newspaper proprietors would succeed in obtaining any information valuable to their readers, and common sense suggested that they should be accordingly enabled to obtain the papers which they wanted by purchasing them. In 1835, therefore, the House of

Commons authorised their sale at a cheap rate. This decision directly led to one of the most memorable struggles which has ever occurred between the law courts and the House. Among the papers which were sold in the first instance, was a report from the Inspectors of Prisons, which incidentally reflected on a book published by Messrs. Stockdale, who were at that time well-known publishers. Stockdale brought an action for libel against Messrs. Hansards, the parliamentary publishers. Lord Denman, the Chief Justice of the Queen's Bench, declared that any one publishing for money matter injurious, or possibly ruinous, to any person, must answer in a court of justice if he is challenged for the libel. The House of Commons, on the contrary, declared that the power of publishing its reports and papers was an essential incident to the constitutional functions of Parliament, and that the institution of a suit before another court on matters affecting the privileges of Parliament was a high breach of privilege. There were no means of reconciling the contrary positions which the House and the Chief Justice thus took up. The conflicts between the two endured for three years. At last Parliament, in 1840, passed a law giving summary protection to persons employed in the publication of parliamentary papers.

The passage of this law closed an important controversy. Papers published under the authority of Parliament were thenceforward privileged just as words spoken in debate were also privileged. But the same reports, if they were printed under independent authority, enjoyed no such protection. A man could not be charged with libel for matter spoken in the House of

Commons; but an action for libel might be brought against the newspaper which published his speech. In the same way Messrs. Hansards were free to publish any parliamentary paper, but the *Times* might be held accountable for venturing to republish it. It so happened, that at the time at which the Stockdale case was before Parliament, an action was brought against the *Times* for publishing some evidence given before a select committee of the Lords on the subject of New Zealand; and the *Times* and the *Post* consequently petitioned that the protection afforded to Hansards might be extended to themselves. Parliament, afraid of creating more "authorised libellers," refused to listen to the petition. In recent times, however, the good sense of Englishmen and the liberal ruling of a judge, have partly remedied the difficulty; Lord Chief Justice Cockburn held that "a newspaper was not liable to an action for libel for the publication of a fair and faithful report of a debate;" and parliamentary reporters may, therefore, prosecute their calling, their employers may print their reports, without fear of the consequences.

It has been the object of the preceding pages to show how the privilege of free speech, originally allowed to the old Anglo-Norman Parliament, and expressly conceded to the House of Commons in Tudor times, has gradually led to the publication of parliamentary reports, the publication of parliamentary papers, and the protection both of reports and papers from actions in the ordinary courts. But it must be recollected that, while these privileges have been gradually established, both Houses of Parliament have steadily maintained their own power to punish offences. This power has frequently been exercised both in the case of their own members as well as in the case of strangers. Wilkes, for instance, was originally expelled from the House of Commons for writing what the House of Commons was pleased to term a seditious libel. Sir F. Burdett was sent to the Tower in 1810 for questioning, in very improper language, the authority of the House of Commons to punish Gale Jones; and O'Connell was reprimanded in 1838 for declaring that a committee of the House of Commons was the most corrupt that ever degraded the administration of justice and the name of the Commons of England. These three examples, drawn from different periods of English history, will sufficiently illustrate the power which the House of Commons has from time to time exercised of punishing its own members. It has concurrently claimed a right to punish other offenders, and this right was not limited to offences against its own privileges. The seventeenth century is full of examples, which Hallam has declared must be reckoned by impartial men as irregularities and encroachments, of the exertion of undue power in the name of privilege. From the infamous case of Floyd—who in 1621 was sentenced by the Lords, on the motion of the Commons, to a brutal punishment, for venturing to reflect on a foreign prince and his wife—to the case of Mist, who in 1721 was sent to Newgate for publishing a Jacobite newspaper, Parliament displayed an unfortunate tendency to notice not merely offences against its own privileges, but cases properly cognisable in the ordinary courts. These pretensions were quietly abandoned after Mist's case; and the House of Commons subsequently contented itself with ordering the attorney-general to prosecute in such matters, instead of proceeding to punish the supposed offender itself. Thenceforward it reserved its own power for its own members or for those who directly or indirectly impugned its authority. The Lords, as a court of record, have punished such offences by fines and by imprisonment. The Commons, since 1666, have committed offenders to the custody of the serjeant-at-arms, to Newgate or to the Tower. The Speaker's warrant, however, expires with the session; and a prorogation, therefore, necessarily releases the offender. In late years commitments of this character have been very rare, and the House has usually been contented with directing the Speaker to reprimand the accused person at the bar. Up to the middle of last century, prisoners exposed to this reprimand, or sentenced to punishment, were forced to kneel. In 1751, however, a man named Murray refused to kneel when ordered to do so; and the Commons, unable to enforce their order, proceeded to declare him guilty of "a high and most dangerous contempt of the authority and privilege of this House." Even in 1751, however, the ideas of parliamentary privilege which were fashionable in St. Stephens, were not popular out of doors. The House had branded Murray with its indignation; the people regarded him as a hero. Some years afterwards the Commons quietly surrendered the absurd claim which Murray had proved was no longer tenable, and persons brought to the bar were allowed to remain standing. The Lords, more tenacious of their privileges, though not more capable of enforcing them, also gave way. Persons reprimanded by the Lords are allowed to stand at the bar; but the entries in the *Lords' Journal* assume that they kneel.

Privilege, as the preceding pages may have shown,

has passed through many phases. Claimed originally by the Commons to help them in their contest with the Crown, it was subsequently used by them in their contest with the people; it fell into comparative disuse when the cause of the nation became the cause of the House of Commons. In the present time no British sovereign would force himself into the legislature and demand the arrest of members obnoxious to himself; but no House of Commons would go out of its way to declare an article in the *Times* a seditious libel, or venture to reprimand the printer of a newspaper who published its debates. Modern sovereigns have had the good sense to refrain from the conduct which cost Charles I. throne and life; and recent Parliaments have had the wisdom to abstain from imitating the examples of the legislatures in the early years of the reign of George III. The supremacy for which the king was contending in the early years of the seventeenth century, and which the House of Commons temporarily obtained in the concluding years of the eighteenth century, has virtually passed to the people, and both the Crown and the aristocracy have practically recognised the facts which it is no longer possible for them to ignore. It would, perhaps, be well for them even now occasionally to reflect on the consequences of the contrary policy which their ancestors pursued. The cause of freedom is the holiest which history commemorates; and the persons who have struck a blow in freedom's cause are the favourite heroes of the historian. In ancient Athens Hipparchus used his power to cultivate wisdom and virtue; Harmodius gave his days to degrading vices; yet the Athenians forgave the one because he slew the other. The private life of George III. was excellent, like that of Hipparchus; the private life of Wilkes was only less degraded than that of Harmodius. Yet Wilkes lives in history as freedom's champion; the government of George III. is condemned as unconstitutional. Callistratus composed his sole surviving lyric in Harmodius' honour; and Byron described in one of his most pungent stanzas the memorable conduct of Wilkes. May future generations take warning from such examples. That policy must at least be unfortunate which holds up rulers such as George III. and Hipparchus to reproach, and which turns characters such as Harmodius and Wilkes into heroes.

CHAPTER VI.

PUBLIC AND PRIVATE BILLS.

THOSE persons who are most intimately acquainted with the history of British industries are best aware of the gradual processes by which machinery has been brought to perfection. The British Parliament is, after all, nothing but a machine, which, simple enough in the first instance, has become more complex as more and more work has been required of it. Those who have read the preceding pages will have some idea of the manner in which the complicated machinery has been gradually produced. But they may still desire to test its capacity in the only manner in which the utility of a machine can be judged—by ascertaining its ability to discharge the duties which it has 'been constructed to perform.

Such an inquiry is essentially necessary at the present moment. Parliamentary institutions are—as we are continually reminded—on their trial. It was the dream of Coningsby to supersede government by Parliament with government by opinion. It was his conviction that two centuries of parliamentary monarchy and parliamentary church had made government detested and religion disbelieved. "Man," wrote Herr Teufelsdröckh a few years before, " is a tool-using animal. He collects, apparently by lot, six hundred and fifty-eight miscellaneous individuals, and says to them, *make this nation toil for us, bleed for us, hunger and sorrow and sin for us;* and they do it." When one of the foremost statesmen and one of the foremost literary men of the age agree in using such language, who can deny that parliamentary institutions are indeed on their trial? Then, since the preceding pages have described the manufacture of the machine, it is high time to pronounce some opinion on its utility.

The work which Parliament has to do is divisible in many ways. Excluding the judicial functions of the House of Lords—with which this book has no concern— the duties of Parliament are partly public and partly private. Public business may be roughly described as work which concerns the entire community. Private business deals with a district, a locality, or an individual. The public business of Parliament may be considered under three distinct heads. Parliament is a legislative machine, a financial machine, and a controlling machine. In the first capacity it makes laws, in the second capacity it grants taxation and regulates expenditure, in the third capacity it controls the executive. These threefold duties of legislation, of taxation, and of supervision have all to be discharged by the 658 gentlemen who, according to Mr. Carlyle, are collected apparently by lot. The utility of Parliament must be tried by the manner in which they are performed.

The legislative functions of Parliament require consideration in the first instance. Since the time of Edward I. the great maxim, "that which touches all shall be approved by all," has regulated legislation in

England; and, though it was occasionally disregarded in Plantagenet times, and frequently neglected by Tudors and Stuarts, the Crown had never power to legislate except by the advice and with the consent of its Parliament. In Plantagenet times legislation was usually adopted on the petition of the Commons, by the advice of the Lords, and with the assent of the sovereign. But this arrangement led to a singular difficulty. The assent of the Crown was not always given in the exact terms in which the petition was framed. Parliament occasionally discovered that, while nominally agreeing to its proposals, the Crown virtually modified its measures. Consequently, in the reign of Henry V., the Crown promised that "henceforth nothing should be enacted to the petitions of the Commons contrary to their asking;" and in the following reign Parliament took the matter into its own hands by superseding petitions and initiating bills.

As a general rule bills can be originated in either House of Parliament. Bills, however, involving a restitution of honours commence with the Lords; bills imposing charges upon the people commence with the Commons. But with these two exceptions either House is competent to originate an Act of Parliament. In the Lords any peer may at once introduce a bill, in the Commons a member must obtain the leave of the House before he can introduce it. When leave is given, the bill is introduced, read a first time, and ordered to be printed. A day is thereupon named for its second reading. After it has been read a second time it is referred to a Committee of the whole House. It is the business of the committee to go through it clause by clause, line by line, and amend it as it thinks proper. The committee reports the amendments which it makes to the House; and the House has then the opportunity either of reconsidering these amendments or of introducing any further amendments which it desires. When these several stages have been completed the bill is read a third time; it is subsequently passed, and carried to the other House. In the other House the same process is gone through. The bill is formally read a first and second time, it is considered in committee, it is reconsidered on the report of the committee. it is read a third time and passed. Should no amendments be made in the House which receives the bill in the last instance the measure is ripe for receiving the Queen's approval. In the more usual case, in which amendments are made, they are referred back for the consideration of the House in which the measure originated. If these amendments are agreed to, the bill receives the royal assent. From that moment the bill becomes an act, its clauses become sections. A change is almost immediately afterwards made in its appearance. Bills are printed on blue, acts on white, paper.

Numerous opportunities thus occur for defeating any bill which is introduced into either House of Parliament. In the case of a Commons' bill, leave may be refused for its introduction; and both Lords' and Commons' bills may be thrown out on the first, on the second, or on the third readings, on the motion that the House do resolve itself into a Committee on the Bill, and on the final motion that the bill do pass. In addition to these opportunities an indefinite number of divisions may be taken on the details of the measure in committee, and fresh amendments, of which due notice must however be given, may lead to fresh discussions on report. Nor, indeed, does this category of occasions, on which opposition is afforded an opportunity of exercising itself, exhaust all the methods by which a bill may be defeated. A motion for reading a bill may be met by a direct negative or by a resolution affirming its inexpediency. The resolution must, in the latter case, be disposed of before the bill can be read. A motion for going into committee is frequently met by a resolution directing the committee to make some particular modifications in the measure, and this motion has to be disposed of before the House can go into committee. During the progress of any debate any member of the House may move the adjournment either of the House or of the debate, and this motion, on which fresh discussions may arise, must be disposed of before the debate can be resumed. The same member may not indeed on the same sitting move the adjournment either of the House or of the debate more than once; but any number of members may severally renew the same motion. The forms of the House, moreover, frequently enable more than one division to take place on the same question. When, for instance, a bill is read a second time, the motion is made "That this bill be now read a second time." A member opposed to the bill proposes to leave the word "now" out of the motion, and the division formally takes place on the technical point whether the word "now" shall or shall not form part of the question. In ordinary cases the decision of the House on this technical point is accepted as conclusive. If the House decides to retain the word "now" it usually reads the bill a second time without further question. If it decides to omit it, it usually allows the words, "on this day six months," or "on this day three months," to be added to the question, which is carried forthwith in its amended shape.

When either House decides on the rejection of a bill, it directs that the bill shall be read on some day six months, three months, or one month afterwards, as the case may be, taking care to name some day on which it is improbable that Parliament will be sitting. The order for the reading of the bill on that day becomes then a lapsed order, and the bill falls through. In divisions the Lords are ranged into Contents and Non-contents, the Commons into "Ayes" and "Noes." Both in the Lords and in the Commons two tellers are appointed on each side to aid the clerks in counting the Ayes and Noes, the Contents and the Non-contents. In both Houses the tellers are named by the Speaker. In both, the Contents and the Ayes go into the right lobby, the Non-contents and the Noes into the left lobby. The names of the members as they pass into the respective lobbies are recorded by clerks, and their numbers are then told by the tellers. The tellers in Parliament, like the now abolished tellers in the Exchequer, derive their names from the old sense of the verb to tell—to count. The tellers in Parliament count votes, the tellers in the Exchequer counted money.

As a matter of fact, leave is usually granted for the introduction of a bill without question. The first reading also is generally passed without debate. But the general practice has occasionally been departed from, and long debates have been raised on· these motions. The debate on the second reading is the most important of the discussions on the bill. The principle of the measure is supposed at that time to be under consideration. The debates on the later stages are usually of less significance. The fate of the bill is practically decided by the divisions which have already taken place; and, as a general rule, the minority recognise their defeat and abstain from further opposition, which cannot affect the result, and which is certain to waste time. Even English members of Parliament, however, occasionally resemble the British troops at Waterloo. They do not know when they are beaten. The British army by their ignorance of what Napoleon considered the rules of war won a great victory. The members usually only waste a great deal of time. When parties, however, are evenly divided, bills have occasionally been defeated on the third reading, and even on the final motion that the bill do pass; and opposition has, therefore, occasionally been protracted with success, if not with advantage, to the very latest stage.

Between the second and third readings, the details of every bill are considered in committee, and the report of the committee is considered in the House. In both Houses, the Speaker in committee leaves the chair; which is then taken in the House of Lords by the chairman of Committee of the whole House, in the House of Commons by the chairman of Committee of Ways and Means. In the Lords the chairman of Committee of the whole House is a peer elected for the purpose at the commencement of every session. In the Commons, the chairman of Committee of Ways and Means is a member elected for the purpose at the commencement of each Parliament. When the House of Commons is in committee, the mace, which usually lies on the table, and which is the symbol of the Speaker's authority, is placed under the table. In both Houses, members in committee may speak an indefinite number of times on each question. The Committee on a Bill terminates its proceedings by reporting that they have gone through the bill and made amendments in it, or made no amendments in it. But when, as usually happens, the labours of a committee are protracted over more than a single sitting, the committee reports "progress" and asks leave to sit again. In committees, therefore, a motion that the chairman do report progress is equivalent to a motion in the House for the adjournment of a debate. A committee cannot adjourn its sitting, as it can only sit by permission of the House.

In the ordinary course, bills referred to a committee are left to the committee's discretion. Occasionally, however, the House instructs the committee to fuse two bills on the same subject into one, or to make some particular amendment in a bill. Occasionally, too, when the bill is manifestly imperfect, or when, for other reasons, its modification is desirable, bills are committed *pro formâ* for the purpose of being reprinted. The member responsible for the bill is thus able to modify his measure without wasting public time. But bills which have thus been reprinted do not escape the committee stage. They are re-committed and formally considered in committee. If the committee makes no alteration in them the House is unable to make any amendment in them on report. If, however, as is more usual, amendments have been made, fresh amendments may be introduced by the House itself on report. On report, however, the ordinary rules of the House are followed: no member can speak more than once to each question, and no amendment can be made of which specific notice has not been given.

Occasionally the House, instead of referring a bill to a Committee of the whole House, sends it, in the first instance, to a Select Committee. Such a course is manifestly convenient in many matters referring to technical questions on which the mass of the House has perhaps only slight information, but with which a certain proportion of its members is well acquainted. Select Committees may be constituted in three ways: by the House itself; by the Committee of Selection; and partly by the House and partly by the Committee of Selection. The Committee of Selection comprises the chairman of the Standing Orders Committee and five other members nominated by the House at the commencement of every session. It owes its name to the fact that it selects the members who are to constitute the Committees on Railway Bills. When a Select Committee is nominated by the House, it usually consists of an equal number of members chosen from both sides of the House and the member on whose motion the nomination is made. In some cases a Select Committee is simply desired to revise a bill; in other cases, in order to enable it to do its work more effectually, it is authorised to send for persons and papers. The committee on a public bill selects its own chairman. The reference to the Select Committee does not do away with the formal consideration of the measure in Committee of the whole House. It merely expedites that stage, since the Committee of the whole House is naturally guided by the opinion of the experienced members to whom the measure has been expressly referred.

Such is the treatment which is or may be accorded to every public bill introduced into either House of Parliament. A bill, however, before it becomes an act, has to receive the assent of both branches of the legislature. Two assemblies, constituted even in the same way, would not always perhaps exhibit a perfect agreement. Two assemblies, composed of such different materials as Lords and Commons, frequently form irreconcilable conclusions. When either the Lords reject a bill which has been passed by the Commons, or the Commons reject a bill which has been passed by the Lords, the issue is simple enough. Unless the matter is one on which a wide interest is felt, the decision of the one House is accepted by the other, and the rejected measure lies dormant till it is revived in another session. In the comparatively rare cases, where the Lords venture to throw out a measure which the public is resolved to obtain, much greater difficulty arises. When the second Reform Bill was rejected by the Lords in 1831, Lord Grey advised the king to prorogue Parliament for a few weeks, in order that a new measure framed on the same principles might be again submitted to the Lords. When an amendment of serious importance was carried in committee, in 1832, on the third Reform Bill, Lord Grey obtained the king's permission if necessary to create peers sufficient for carrying his measure. When, in 1860, the Lords rejected the Paper Duties Repeal Bill, the Commons determined in future to comprise the whole of the financial arrangements of each year in one bill; and, as the Lords are not at liberty to reject a money bill, compel the peers to accept the scheme or refuse it as a whole. The student of constitutional history will probably observe, indeed, that every occasion, which the Lords have taken for asserting their independence on a really vital question, has been attended with a sensible diminution of their authority; and statesmen will probably deduce from this circumstance that the ultimate extinction of the peers as hereditary legislators, if it should take place at all, will be due to their own inability to reconcile their conduct to the requirements of the age in which they are living.

There are, however, comparatively few measures which are accepted by one House and rejected by the other. In the great majority of cases the issue is a much smaller one. One House introduces an amendment which the other does not approve. Both are willing to accept the measure, but both desire it in a form more or less different. Practical men, on such occasions, usually attempt a compromise. The matters in dispute between Lords and Commons are frequently compromised. But compromise requires communication; and this fact necessitates an explanation of the manner in which communications between the two Houses can take place.

In ordinary cases, when one House of Parliament wishes to communicate with the other, it sends a message. Up to a very recent period the Lords used to send their messages to the Commons by two Masters in Chancery, or, in the case of bills relating to the royal family, by two judges; the Commons used to send their messages to the Lords by eight members, of whom the chairman of Committee of Ways and Means was usually one. Modern habits are opposed to unnecessary ceremony, and forms, which in our fathers' time were regarded with respect, in our own time only produce ridicule. During the last quarter of a century each House has, except on rare occasions, sent its messages by one of its clerks; and the obvious utility of this practice has insured its general adoption. When one House refuses to accept the amendments which the other has introduced into a bill, it was, till thirty years ago, the usual practice to demand a conference. A conference can only be demanded by the House in possession of the matter in dispute, or, in other words, by the House to which the unacceptable amendments have been returned; it can be refused if the demand for it should not specifically state the subjects to be discussed at it. When once accepted, the time and place of meeting at the conference are fixed by the Lords. Both Houses appoint managers to represent them at the conference. But the managers have duties of the merest ceremony to discharge. The managers, of the House which demands the conference, hand in reasons for disagreeing from the amendments which are objected to. The managers of the other House report these reasons to those whom they represent. If this ceremony be successful in terminating the difference, the objectionable amendments are withdrawn. If, on the contrary, the House which has introduced the amendments remains firm, a second conference can be held. But, if the second conference should prove as abortive as the first, it used to be the habit to demand a free conference. A free conference was attended by all the members of both Houses; the Commons arrived at the place appointed first, and stood uncovered throughout the meeting. The Lords arrived afterwards, and, after uncovering for a moment, sat covered. The managers on each side, instead of formally communicating written reasons, were "at liberty to urge their own arguments," and the conference accordingly led to an informal, spiritless debate. The antiquated ceremony was of course usually useless. Members, who had clung to their own opinions throughout the long stages through which every measure passes, were not likely to be converted by arguments addressed to them by speakers of a strange assembly. The free conference, with its curious formalities, has consequently fallen into disuse: only one free conference has been held since 1740; no free conference has been held since 1836. Even the ordinary conference has of late years been rarely held; and legislators have discovered that it is more convenient to send its messages by a messenger, than to communicate them at a conference.

If conferences or messages fail to reconcile the differences of the two Houses, the measure is lost. If, on the other hand, the two Houses succeed in coming to an agreement, the measure is ripe for the sovereign's approval. Technically the Crown is still at liberty to refuse assent to a bill. In practice the Crown has not refused its assent since the reign of Anne; and it is impossible to anticipate that its assent will ever be refused. The Crown can only act on the advice of its responsible ministers. The responsible ministers of the Crown are dependent on the favour of the House of Commons, and no ministry could accordingly advise the Crown to reject a measure which the House of Commons had passed. In the old days, when the sovereign's power was greater, and when he occasionally exercised the right of rejecting measures, he did so by using the cautious words, "Le Roi s'avisera." In assenting to a measure, the old formula, "Le Roi" or "La Reine le veult," is still used. But the Crown's assent to a bill granting money is given more graciously, "La Reine remercie ses bons sujets, accepte leur benevolence, et ainsi le veult." The Crown's assent to a private bill is given in the words, "Soit fait comme il est désiré."

In addition to the public bills which Parliament annually considers, it has simultaneously to deal with a constantly increasing mass of private legislation. In theory the private bill receives the same treatment as the public bill. In practice, however, it is dealt with in a totally different way, and therefore, in such a work as this, requires separate consideration.

Up to 1798, the distinction which the Statute Book now draws between general and local acts was not observed. Public acts affecting the whole community, and local acts affecting only portions of it, were printed together, and personal acts were alone printed separately. Since 1798, however, all local and personal acts have been excluded from the general list of statutes. The public acts have been ranged in the order in which they pass each session, and numbered with an ordinary Arabic number. The local and personal, or private acts, have been ranged in similar order, and numbered with a Roman numeral. For instance, to take a comparatively recent example, the Army Discipline and Regulation Act, 1879, is numbered the 42nd and 43rd Victoria, caput 33. It is the thirty-third act or chapter of the public statute passed in the session of Parliament which commenced in the forty-second and concluded in the forty-third year of her Majesty's reign. The 42nd & 43rd Victoria, caput ccxix., is a local act authorising the Crown to sell a strip of land at Knightsbridge to the Metropolitan Board of Works. It is the 219th private act passed in the same session. In common speech, however, people do not talk of the 42 & 43 Victoria, caput 33, or of the 42 & 43 Victoria, cap. ccxix. These numbers are chiefly used to indicate the position which each act occupies in the Statute Book. Of late years Parliament has usually inserted a short title in the body of the act itself by which it may be known. The 42 & 43 Victoria, caput 33, may, for instance, be recited even in parliamentary documents as the Army Discipline and Regulation Act, 1879. In ordinary conversation the title would be further—though inaccurately—abbreviated; and the act would be styled the Army Discipline Act.

Up to 1798, the acts printed as private acts were exclusively personal. They arranged the divorces of rich men and women who did not happen to agree, the naturalisation of wealthy foreigners, and other like matters. But a demand was already arising for other legislation of a more important nature—for the making of roads or of canals, for the erection of bridges, for the construction of harbours, for the management of towns, for the paving or lighting of different places, and for other things. Much of this legislation has, in its turn, become unnecessary, and, at the present time, the most important private legislation deals with railways. One hundred years ago private bills mostly dealt with personal requirements; fifty years ago they chiefly promoted local or parochial objects. The most important private legislation now authorises undertakings of national importance.

Private legislation, it need hardly be stated, requires treatment different from public legislation. To take the simplest case: an act authorising a company to make a railway raises issues distinct from those in an act for licensing public-houses or for providing education for the people. In the one case Parliament has only to consider what arrangements are best for the public good; in the other case it has concurrently to guard against injustice being inadvertently done to any individual. The promoters of a railway do not come before the legislature as public benefactors; they have a direct pecuniary interest in the scheme which they are promoting. The opposition to a railway, again, is not usually based on public grounds. The opponents are generally concerned with their private interest. In rejecting or accepting the scheme, therefore, Parliament does something more than legislate for the public good. It determines a private issue. It acts not merely in a legislative capacity, it concurrently assumes judicial functions. As a legislature it still observes its ordinary forms of proceeding, but, as a court of law, it insists on other additional observances.

The rules to which the promoters of a private bill have to attend are complicated. A petition for a private bill must be deposited in the Private Bill Office before the 21st December. Before that date the promoters of the bill must have complied with the Standing Orders of both Houses of Parliament. These orders require that the bill shall be duly advertised; that notice shall be duly given to the owners and occupiers of all property affected by it; that the documents referred to in the scheme shall be deposited in duly appointed places; that the plans, &c., illustrating these documents shall be prepared in duly specified forms; that estimates of the cost of the proposed works shall be prepared; and that, in certain cases, a proportion of the money required shall be lodged with a duly nominated authority. It is the duty of two officers, the examiners of private bills, appointed by the House of Lords and the Speaker of the House of Commons, to ascertain and report whether the Standing Orders have been complied with. In the case of unopposed bills the examiner merely reports his decision on this point. In the case of opposed bills he hears, before pronouncing his decision, any complaints of non-compliance. But, opposed or unopposed, every private bill is subjected to this preliminary ordeal before one of the two examiners of private bills.

When the petition for a private bill has been duly endorsed by the examiners, the petition for the bill must be presented to the House by some member in charge of it. If the examiner has reported that the Standing Orders have been complied with, the House at once directs the bill to be introduced. If the examiner has reported that the Standing Orders have not been complied with, the petition of the bill is referred, with the examiner's report, to a committee of eleven members, chosen each session, and known as the Standing Orders' Committee. It is the duty of this committee to determine whether the Standing Orders should be enforced or dispensed with, and whether the bill should be allowed to proceed. If the committee report that the Standing Orders should be enforced, the bill is, as a general rule, lost. If, on the contrary, it reports that the Standing Orders should be dispensed with, the member in charge of the bill moves that the report of the committee be read, and that leave be given to introduce the bill. The second reading of the bill is fixed for a day not less than three and not more than seven days after its first reading. As a general rule the second reading of a private bill is passed without debate as a matter of form, and the bill is then referred to a committee. Occasionally, however, the House adopts the less usual course of discussing the principle of the bill on its second reading, and private bills have been rejected by Parliament at this stage.

The private bill, which has been read a second time, is referred either to the Committee of Selection, or, in the case of railways and canals, to the General Committee on Railway and Canal Bills. These committees, which are both appointed at the commencement of each session, perform analogous duties. They arrange private bills into groups, and refer each group to the consideration of a committee. It is again easiest to confine the attention to a particular case. The General Committee on Railway and Canal Bills would probably refer the bills relating to the metropolis to one committee; the bills affecting Scotland to a second; and so on. Each committee consists of four members and a referee. One member, who is chairman of the committee, is appointed by and is himself a member of the General Committee on Railway and Canal Bills; the three other members are chosen by the Committee of Selection. The members serving on the committee must have no personal or local interest in the bill; their attendance is compulsory; and they are required to sign a declaration that they will not vote on any matter without having duly heard and attended to the evidence thereon.

The committee which is thus constituted is charged with the duty of examining the case for and against the private bill. The case for the bill is stated by its promoters; the case against it by petitioners against it. No petitioner is entitled to be heard unless he has a *locus standi* on which to base his petition. The *locus standi* of a petitioner is decided in the Commons by the Court of Referees, a tribunal consisting of the chairman of Ways and Means, and at least three officers nominated by the Speaker; in the Lords by the committee to which the bill is referred. The promoters and petitioners are represented before the committee by counsel; the witnesses, on either side, are examined on oath; and the forms customary in judicial proceedings are observed. The committee is required ultimately to report in favour of or against the bill. If a bill is adopted by the committee the report technically runs that its preamble is proved. But the proof of the preamble is only one step in the labours of the committee. It becomes its immediate duty to consider the bill itself. The struggle on the bill may raise many more issues than the struggle on the preamble, since many petitioners, who have no interest in the bill generally, may be affected by particular clauses, and consequently entitled to a hearing. The committee, after hearing the evidence, may amend the bill by either enlarging it or restricting it, as it thinks proper. On the completion of its labours its chairman reports its decision to the House. The House appoints a day for the consideration of the bill, when it may either be amended or recommitted. As a general rule, however, the other stages of the bill are purely formal, and the bill, as a matter of course, is read a third time and passed.

It must not be supposed that this account of the ordeal, to which every private bill is exposed, exhausts all the opportunities which exist for disputing its progress. A bill which has passed the Commons has to go through the same ordeal in the Lords; a bill which has passed the Lords has to go through the same ordeal in the Commons. In the preceding narrative, the course pursued by the Commons has been specially kept in view; but the procedure adopted by the Lords varies only slightly from that adopted by the Commons.

It is hardly necessary to say that proceedings of this character, repeated on two separate occasions, naturally involve a great expense. The promoters of a bill and the petitioners against it have to employ agents and counsel to represent them. They are compelled to bring their witnesses to London; to maintain them in the metropolis; and frequently to pay them large sums of money for their attendance; and they have to repeat the process twice over in the same session. It may be some small consolation to these gentlemen to reflect that, in the early days of railways, the composition of committees was more elaborate, and the proceedings before them more costly. Ordinary people, however, are not satisfied to tolerate an inconvenience because it nappens to be less marked than in the days of their fathers. A strong feeling exists in many circles against the expense and difficulties which surround the passage of every private measure; and it may safely be predicted that the present system must sooner or later perish and be replaced by some simpler machinery.

It is not difficult to determine the form which new machinery must assume. Parliament has gradually relieved itself of many duties, and the same process of relief will be continued. Within the memory of many persons still alive, no divorce could be obtained and no foreigner could be naturalized except by a private act. Within the recollection of persons who are still young, every petition against a contested election was referred to a Select Committee of the House of Commons. For the last thirty-five years a Secretary of State has been empowered to grant a certificate of naturalization. For the last four-and-twenty years a court has been constituted to dissolve marriages. For the last dozen years the ordinary judges have been allowed to try election petitions; and experience has proved that these administrative and legislative changes have relieved Parliament of a good deal of incongruous labour, and have conferred great advantages on the public. In the same way, till within a comparatively recent period, a county which required a police force, a town which desired to provide for its own poor, a company which demanded incorporation, a landlord who wished to sell an entailed estate, had no alternative but to seek legislative sanction. In all these cases, public acts passed in the interest of the entire community have saved the necessity of private legislation. Successful experiments are certain to be imitated. Up to 1845 every inclosure of common land had been effected by a private Act of Parliament. In 1845 Commissioners were appointed authorised to conduct the inclosures themselves. It is the duty of these gentlemen to inquire into the whole of the circumstances connected with the inclosure, and to frame, if they think proper to sanction it, an order authorizing it to be made. The order, however, does not come into force until after it has been confirmed by Parliament, and, as it is provisional on such confirmation, it is called a Provisional Order. It is the duty of the Secretary of State for the Home Department to lay annually before Parliament some short bill asking for the confirmation of these orders;

and these bills are subjected to the ordinary ordeal which every public Act of Parliament undergoes. Parliament, therefore, does not in any way part with the check which it possesses on inclosures; it merely deputes a public office to conduct an inquiry, which, in other days, it would have itself conducted through the instrumentality of a Select Committee. A public office can of course direct one of its officers to go into the neighbourhood of the inclosure, and to take the evidence which may be required on the subject on the spot. It can thus avoid the expense and inconvenience of bringing a host of witnesses to London and of maintaining them in the metropolis. The simple expedient, therefore, of a provisional order—capable of being inforced only on its confirmation by Parliament—has been productive of convenience and economy, without diminishing the control of the legislature.

The system which is most easily illustrated by the example of inclosures, has been applied since to piers, harbours, tramways, fisheries, and many other purposes. The invention of provisional orders may, indeed, be almost said to have superseded the necessity for private-bill legislation in the case of the smaller local schemes. It may be confidently predicted that the extension of the system will, some day or other, supersede the necessity for all private legislation whatever. It ought to be easy to form in each of the three kingdoms some competent tribunal, capable of inquiring into the expediency of all schemes submitted for the approval of the legislature, and of framing provisional orders for the sanction of Parliament. A judge, assisted by a competent assessor, or assessors, would, for instance, in most cases form a satisfactory tribunal; while any tribunal sitting on the spot must—other things being equal—be more satisfactory than a tribunal sitting at a distance. The great question of Home Rule, in its broad and popular sense, may on some future day become a pressing matter. But Home Rule, in the limited sense in which it is contemplated in this paragraph, ought to be an object for every fair politician to desire.

From what has already been written it will thus be seen that in private business as in other matters two distinct processes have been going on. The old kinds of business which used to occupy the attention of Parliament—divorce bills, naturalisation bills, inclosure bills, and others—have been removed from Parliament by administrative and legislative reforms, and the invention of provisional orders, while the introduction of railways has forced the legislature to deal with a new kind of business of infinitely greater importance than the old. The change of jurisdiction thus effected, like every other change, was not adopted without hesitation or carried without opposition. Many persons, whose benevolence exceeded their judgment, shrank from intrusting large powers to commissioners whom they regarded as irresponsible; or from committing to a public department powers which had been hitherto exercised by the legislature alone. But the convenience which resulted from the reform soon afforded a practical answer to scruples of this character. It was rightly concluded that much of the work which was taken from Parliament was more economically and more efficiently conducted than before; and the legislature obtained the concurrent advantage of relief from embarrassing functions of no general interest, and was able to devote the time, which it thus saved, to other and more comprehensive duties.

K

CHAPTER VII.

SUPPLY.

A BOOK, professing to deal with an electorate and a legislature, has naturally to direct attention in the first instance to the legislative functions of the British Parliament. But Parliament, it must be recollected, is not a mere legislature, but a Parliament. As a Parliament it has other and perhaps more important duties than those of legislation to discharge. Foremost among these is the right which it possesses to impose taxation and control expenditure.

Ever since the statute of 1297 the undoubted right of taxation has rested with the representatives of those who bore the burden. The three estates voted their scutages and aids separately; but it naturally resulted from this circumstance that the estate which represented the nation acquired the power of the purse. The contribution of the many was much more important than the grants of the few; and the Commons accordingly gradually claimed the sole right of initiating taxation. "The customs and privileges of this (the Commons) House," said Bacon, "hath always been first to make offer of the subsidies from hence, then to the Upper House." The supplies, in the phraseology of a modern writer, were always granted by the Commons and assented to by the Lords. And this radical difference between the functions of the two Houses has led to a striking parenthesis in the speech which the sovereign periodically delivers, either personally or by commissioners, from the throne. She addresses through the bulk of her speech, Peers and Commoners, Lords and Gentlemen; but those paragraphs of her speech which refer to taxation she addresses to the gentlemen of the House of Commons alone.

The Commons, then, have the sole right of granting taxation. It is obvious that any public body must be incompetent to determine the taxation which will be necessary until it has accurately ascertained the expenditure which is requisite. It is a primary rule with the House of Commons that it will not sanction any grant of public money which is not recommended to it by the Crown. Technically, therefore, the ministers of the Crown are responsible for the initiation of all expenditure; and so strictly is this rule followed that cases have occurred in which addresses recommending expenditure have been carried, and have led to no results. The ministers of the Crown have refused to move, and the House of Commons has proved unable to compel them to do so.

It is the practice of the ministers of the Crown, soon after the commencement of each session, to lay before the House of Commons estimates of the expenditure of the ensuing financial year. These estimates are comprised in three volumes: one relating to the army, a second to the navy, a third to the civil service. They contain a full account of the expenditure of the nation. Every service, with its exact cost, is placed under separate heads; and the House of Commons thus obtains an express control over the whole expenditure of the country. These estimates are considered, item by item, or, in House of Commons phraseology, vote by vote, in what is called Committee of Supply. In committee every member is entitled to take exception to any item in the estimates, to move its omission or reduction, or to question its expediency. Some of the most interesting debates in the whole session arise in Committee of Supply. Professed economists, indeed, occasionally doubt whether the game is quite worth the candle. One man, who devoted a whole lifetime to criticising estimates, is said to have declared that he had never in any single instance succeeded in defeating a vote. The estimates are in fact framed with such care, and the Treasury enforces retrenchment with such persistency, that there are comparatively few items left in the estimates to which it is possible for any one to take exception. Room for economy, indeed, still remains; but economy in future must obviously be sought by new methods. It is by the rearrangement of administration, and not by the criticism of details, that money is to be saved. The economical reformers by their petty conduct have made even economy unpopular; the administrative reformer has not yet arisen to restore it to popularity.

The estimates, however, are agreed to vote by vote, item by item, in Committee of Supply. The House of Commons has determined that money voted for one purpose may not be applied to another; and the money, therefore, voted in the estimates, is intrusted to the minister for the specific purposes for which it is granted. A rule of this kind is admirable; yet it may be reasonably doubted whether it has not been made the fertile excuse for extravagance. Ministers plausibly say that they are not in all cases able to foresee in January all the demands which will be made on their departments in the course of the year. A habit has in consequence arisen of supplementing the estimates which are presented at the commencement of the session with further estimates towards its close, and occasionally with still further estimates at the commencement of the following year. This practice has the advantage of exactness, but it has the disadvantage of concealing the growth of expenditure from nine men out of every ten in Parliament, and from ninety-nine men out of every hundred in the country. The gross amount of all the estimates in the beginning of one year is placed at (say) £50,000,000; it is raised to £50,500,000 before the close of the session; and to £50,750,000 before the commencement of another session. The estimates for the following year are placed at £50,500,000, and the ministers are able to take credit for an apparent reduction of £250,000; and conceal the real growth of £500,000, which has taken place in the twelve months. It is not too much to say that, with few exceptions, for years past ministers have been crediting themselves with decreases of this character, while the expenditure of the country has been going on, almost uniformly, increasing.

Economical reformers could not attempt a more useful task than the simplification of the estimates. But economical reform does not fall within the limits of this book, which is rather concerned with the method in which Parliament deals with the estimates, than with the manner in which they are framed. The Commons, it has already been stated, agree to the estimates vote by vote in Committee of Supply. The committee reports its decisions to the House; and the resolutions, agreed to in committee, are then confirmed. Towards the end of the session the whole of the votes which are thus adopted are included in a bill which recites in its schedules all the supplies which the House of Commons has agreed to grant to the Crown. Since the supplies which are thus voted can only be applied to the specific objects for which they are granted, this bill is known as the Appropriation Bill. The Appropriation Bill runs through the ordinary stages of other acts of Parliament. But, as it covers almost the whole expenditure of the year, and deals consequently with a great variety of subjects, the discussion on it need not necessarily be confined to the subject of supply, but may turn upon almost any subject which is embraced in the bill.

The Appropriation Bill deals with all the supplies voted in the year for the service of the year. Its schedules, therefore, contain the best short abstract of the estimated cost of the Supply Services. In addition to these charges, however, which are sanctioned for only a limited period of twelve months, Parliament from time to time sanctions other charges for longer periods. The chief of them are: (1) the charge of the National Debt, and (2) the other charges on what is known as the Consolidated Fund. The greater portion of the former could not be refused without a breach of faith, and much of the latter consists of items which it would be undesirable to subject to annual discussion. The charge of the debt has during the last few years been divided into two portions. The largest of these includes a fixed sum for the payment of the interest on what Parliament is pleased inaccurately to style the Permanent Debt, and for the Sinking Fund; the smaller of them deals with a smaller sum for the payment of the interest on what, almost as inaccurately, Parliament is pleased to call the Temporary Debt. These sums are fixed from time to time by separate acts of Parliament, the last of which was only passed in the present year. The other charges on the Consolidated Fund embrace a variety of items which have been granted from time to time by Parliament. The most important of these is the Civil List of the sovereign, fixed at the commencement of the reign at £385,000, and the pensions which have been granted since to the sovereign's children or relatives. In addition to these charges, however, the descendants of distinguished subjects, such as the Duke of Marlborough and Duke of Wellington, are entitled either for ever or for terms of lives to pensions on the Consolidated Fund. Many persons still living, eminent for their services to the state in the field, on the Bench, or in Parliament, are similarly entitled to pensions; and other persons without any claims but the good fortune or the light conduct of their ancestors have been similarly rewarded. In addition to these pensioners, the salaries of some of the higher officials of the state, such as the Speaker of the House of Commons, are charged on the Consolidated Fund. Parliament has seen fit to fix and vote these items once for all instead of subjecting them to annual revision.

The expenditure of the nation is thus divided into two portions. First, certain portions of it which have been voted by Parliament and do not require periodical revision; and second, other portions of it, voted from year to year, which are annually approved. The revenue of the country is susceptible of similar divisions. Some taxes are voted either in perpetuity or for long periods of years, while others are only granted for short periods of one or two years. Whether, however, the particular tax be voted for a long or for a short period, the same procedure is followed. Once a year the whole of the financial arrangements are reviewed by the House of Commons. The Chancellor of the Exchequer explains to the House the proposals which he intends to make. As the financial year commences on the 1st of April, the explanation is usually given on the first convenient day after that date. It is called the budget from the French word *bogette*, a bag ; and the budget is introduced, or the financial statement is made, in committee. When the House is dealing with the estimates it resolves itself into a Committee of Supply. When it is considering the manner in which the supply shall be raised it resolves into a Committee of Ways and Means. The Chancellor of the Exchequer, therefore, usually brings forward his budget in Committee of Ways and Means, and resolutions embodying the budget proposals are adopted in this committee. These resolutions are duly reported to the House, and the House orders bills to be founded on them and submitted for its approval. These bills pass through the stages required in the case of other acts of Parliament.

Two things will probably be clear from the foregoing sketch. First, the details of the expenditure of the year are annually settled in a committee known as the Committee of Supply, and embodied in a bill known as the Appropriation Bill. Second, the ways and means for raising the necessary revenue are annually considered in a committee known as the Committee of

Ways and Means, and also embodied in one or more bills. The decision of the House of Commons in committee is therefore subject to review and to the approval of both Houses of Parliament and the Crown. The House of Commons is technically able to amend an Appropriation Bill or a Supply Bill in its passage through the House in any way that it thinks proper. But the House of Lords has no such power. It may accept the Bill as a whole, or it may reject it as a whole; but it is not at liberty to amend it. The limited power which the Lords thus possess in the case of money bills has been clearly understood since the end of the fourteenth century. Since the reign of Charles I. the matter has been made still more plain; and the preamble of Supply Bills has recited the grant as the gift of the Commons alone, adding the usual words to show that the enactment was passed with the assent of both Houses of the legislature.

It is not clear that the Lords were not originally able to amend a money bill sent up to them. Their right to do so was first denied by the Commons in the reign of Charles II. They have since steadily persisted in this denial, and the Lords have for some time past acquiesced in it. The most eminent constitutional historian, whom this country has yet produced, was not able to reconcile himself to the manner in which the Commons' claim was made, or to justify the making of it. But most thinkers would probably agree that the convenience of the rule forms the best apology for it. For more than two centuries the Lords have not ventured to amend a money bill. But it was perhaps naturally assumed that, though they had no power of amending a money bill, they still retained the right of rejecting it. The right, however, if it existed, was suffered to lapse, and its existence was almost forgotten. In 1860, however, the Commons, in revising the financial arrangements of the year, decided on repealing an excise on paper. A bill repealing the tax was passed through all its stages and sent to the Lords, and the Lords determined to reject it. Nothing perhaps which the Lords had done since their rejection of the second Reform Bill in 1831 had excited so general a feeling of indignation. Many persons thought that if the Lords had the right to reject a bill repealing taxation they virtually exercised the right of imposing taxation, since they continued a tax which the Commons had determined to remit. Lord Palmerston, however, who was Prime Minister at the time, had the discretion to refer the matter to a committee, with instructions to search for precedents, and thus allow time for passion to cool. The committee discovered that on certain occasions the Lords had exercised the right of rejecting tax bills, though they had prudently foreborne from exercising it for a long period. Armed with this report, Lord Palmerston proposed a series of resolutions affirming the rights of the Commons and declaring that they had in their hands the power so to impose and remit taxes and to frame bills of supply that the right of the Commons may be maintained inviolate. In accordance with this declaration, in the following session the whole financial arrangements of the year, including the repeal of the paper duty, were included in one bill and sent up to the Lords. The Lords could not obviously upset the whole financial arrangements of the year, and they were accordingly compelled to pass the bill and to submit to the repeal of the paper duties. Since that time the same precedent has been adopted, and the whole of the financial arrangements of the year have been included in one bill, and the Lords have virtually been rendered powerless in financial matters.

The device by which the action of the Lords in 1860 was defeated in 1861 was no novel expedient. In former ages the Commons on more than one occasion had "tacked" a bill, which they thought the Lords would not accept, to a money bill, and so compelled them to pass an obnoxious measure or to refuse the king his supply. The device was adopted on one notable occasion at the close of the seventeenth century, and William III.'s favourites were forced to disgorge the grants which had been made to them out of the Irish forfeited lands by an act compelling them to do so tacked to a money bill. The gross extravagance which the king had displayed, and the inability of the Commons to frustrate his policy in any other way, are the only possible excuses for a policy which was certainly novel, and which was perhaps unconstitutional. A repetition of the same experiment at the commencement of the reign of Anne was less successful. The Lords resolved "that the annexing any clause or clauses to a bill of aid or supply, the matter of which is foreign to, or different from, the matter of the said bill of aid or supply, is unparliamentary, and tends to the destruction of the constitution of this government." Appalled by this resolution, the Commons gave way; and, though they subsequently renewed the same experiment, the Lords again stood firm. Tacking ceased to be possible from the attitude of the Upper House, and in this century only one instance of it has occurred. It may be hoped that the House of Commons may never have occasion to subject the constitution to so violent a strain as the resumption of this expedient would involve. But it is obvious that the weapon remains in their hands; that, since the decision of 1861 to comprise the whole financial arrangements of the year in one act, it has become much more formidable; and that, in the event of an irreconcilable difference between the two Houses, it might form a possible expedient by which the Commons might control the Lords.

It has already been shown that all grants of money and all votes in supply originate in committee. The House of Commons cannot resolve itself into committee without an express motion; and the proposal to do so, therefore, affords an opportunity for debate, which the rules of the House enable to turn on any conceivable subject. Technically, the debate arises in this way. A member of the Government proposes "That the Speaker do now leave the chair" for the House to go into committee. The words "That the Speaker do now leave the chair" form the question before the House. But any member in the House may propose the omission of all the words after the word "that," in order that other words, for instance, "the conduct of the Secretary of State for the Home Department in issuing a warrant to open letters passing through the post deserves the censure of the House," may be substituted. A division is then taken on the question that the words proposed to be left out stand part of the question. If the question is carried in the affirmative the House resolves that the original motion shall be put that the Speaker do now leave the chair. If, on the contrary, it is carried in the negative, the House proceeds to substitute this amendment, "the conduct of the Secretary of State for the Home Department in issuing a warrant to open letters passing through the post deserves the censure of the House." On supply nights, that is, on nights when the House resolves itself into a Committee of Supply, a long string of motions of this character is usually placed on the notice paper. Discussions upon them are only limited when a division takes place on one of them and the motion is disposed of. When this occurs the House immediately addresses itself to the main question that the Speaker do now leave the chair, and the next division accordingly lands it in committee.

The system of intercepting motions for Committees of Supply and Ways and Means by debates of this character may seem unnecessarily inconvenient to a modern reader. The student of English history, on the contrary, may be tempted to attach an undue importance to it. In the bad periods of autocratic government the sovereigns of England would rarely have resorted to the expedient of summoning a Parliament if they had not required pecuniary assistance, which it was impossible for them to obtain in any other way. But Parliament uniformly refused to vote a supply until the grievances of which it complained were redressed, or, at any rate, until it obtained a promise that they would be remedied. There was a time when the refusal of the Crown to give way, on the one hand, and the determination of the House of Commons to grant no supply till the Crown gave way, on the other, almost reduced parliamentary government to a dead lock. But the Commons risked the consequences of standing firm, and the Crown was ultimately compelled to yield. Its concession usually secured a liberal reward; the assent of Charles I., for instance, to the Petition of Right was immediately followed by the grant of five subsidies, a sum probably equal to £350,000 or £400,000.

A long struggle between Parliament and the Crown convinced the House of Commons that the refusal of the supplies constituted the stoutest weapon in its armoury, and that mere postponement of a money grant could usually bring the executive to reason. The Crown had made it apparent that it would do nothing except upon compulsion, and that the only method by which the Commons could secure attention to their demands was a steady refusal of pecuniary assistance to the king. The maxim consequently arose—the redress of grievances must precede supply; and the maxim is still repeated under conditions which have deprived it of its original significance. But an adherence to the old rule—though it has lost its former meaning—is still of importance. The House of Commons has no longer occasion to dread the arbitrary conduct of the monarch, but it has still reason to maintain its firm control over the executive. To enable it to do so it is essential that it should be able to force on the discussion of any subject; and the old rule that grievances shall precede supply thus obtains a new reason for its existence.

CHAPTER VIII.

ORDER AND OBSTRUCTION.

HE who has studied most carefully the procedure of Parliament, who has obtained the fullest knowledge of the mass of business which it has annually to transact, and who has the most acquaintance with the opportunities which its forms afford for opposition, or even for delay, will perhaps, instead of marvelling at the block of business which contemporary critics deplore, be disposed to wonder at the amount of work which the legislature, in some way or another, manages to get through. In the session of 1878-9, for instance, the last regular session of the last Parliament, the House of Commons sat for 1,148 hours. But in those 1,148 hours it succeeded in passing 222 public and 225 private acts of Parliament. The preceding sections of this work will have shown that legislation is only one of many duties thrown on the House of Commons. But, even assuming that the whole 1,148 hours had been devoted to the work of legislation alone, it is obvious that the 447 public and private acts of Parliament, the legislative results of the session, could only have occupied a little over two hours and a half apiece. But, of course, in reality a large portion of the session was occupied with other business. It is perhaps impossible to say exactly how much time was absorbed by the questioning of ministers, by the discussion of motions, by consideration of the estimates in Committee of Supply, and of the budget in the Committee of Ways and Means, and by debating other legislative proposals which were either defeated or abandoned. But, on the assumption, which is perhaps reasonable, that one hour out of every three may be thus accounted for, it is plain that about 760 out of the 1,148 hours were only available for the work of successful legislation. In that case the 447 public and private acts of Parliament, which were the outcome of the session, instead of occupying on an average two and a half hours each, only in reality absorbed about one hour and three quarters apiece.

A statistical fact of this kind is not without significance. Nine men out of every ten in England, who take an interest in politics, confine their attention to three or four prominent subjects each session. They watch, in common with their fellow countrymen, the progress of these measures; they are vexed, in common with their fellow countrymen, at the obstacles which frequently arrest them; and they are amazed at the almost interminable repetition of the same arguments, by politicians whose only claim to a hearing is that they have secured the confidence of a more or less numerous body of electors. On these occasions the observer is driven to the conclusion that Parliament is overwhelmed by a mere sea of talk. But, when, as occasionally occurs, talk is used as an engine of obstruction, the observer hastily concludes that the whole machine has hopelessly broken down. He sees the difficulty of passing one measure; he is ignorant of the statistics demonstrating the ease with which the 446 other measures are disposed of. Yet the conclusion which he consequently forms is evidently erroneous. No one would dream of saying that the Court of Queen's Bench was hopelessly incompetent to perform its work because it had devoted a period of many weeks to investigating a single memorable case. It would be immediately answered that it had disposed of dozens of other cases in as many minutes as it had devoted hours to the Tichborne difficulty. Exactly in the same way, the long debates on Ireland, which arrest every one's attention, do not necessarily prove that the legislative machine is at a standstill. The legislative machine, on the contrary, in the vast majority of cases, goes on working as smoothly as ever. It is only in exceptional instances that it breaks hopelessly down.

Obstruction, moreover, deplorable as it is from one point of view, is only a symptom of the increasing importance of the House of Commons. The Tory, as well as the Radical, is convinced that the battle of the constitution can only be fought in that House. It is daily becoming more and more impossible to trust the Lords to throw out a measure which the country is resolute in desiring, and which the Tories cannot succeed in defeating in the Commons. The minority, if it fight at all, must confine its efforts to the Lower House. In politics, as well as in warfare, men will place themselves under a Fabius till they find an opportunity for ranging themselves under a Nero; and they will arrest the progress of measures, which they are unable to defeat, by a policy of delay. So Burke, a century ago, resisted the proposal of the Onslows for punishing the reporters; so the Tories, half a century ago, resisted the passage of the Reform Bill of 1831; so the Irish, in Peel's second ministry, delayed for months the passage of an Arms Bill; so the Conservatives, within the last few years, met the proposal for abolishing purchase in our army; so the Irish, in the last few months, have opposed the application of coercion to Ireland. The Tories, who are indignant with the Home Rulers in 1881, forget that they are only following to its extreme the precedent which was set them by the Whigs under Burke, and the Tories under Croker and Wetherell. They are adopting, like Fabius, the policy of delay. They have, at least, enough wisdom to avoid precipitating defeat by decisive divisions.

Delay, then, carried to the utmost extent which the forms of Parliament allow, is the shield which a resolute minority will inevitably use, and their resolution to use it is an admission on their part that the House of Commons, and the House of Commons alone, is virtually supreme. No one ventures on obstruction in the House of Lords, because it is worth no one's while to do so. The House of Lords, in consequence, transacts its business with an ease and a rapidity which the House of Commons may well envy. Its members are usually able to adjourn in time for dinner. They frequently have literally nothing to do. So rare an event as a midnight sitting does not occur half-a-dozen times a year. Yet the House of Lords is a branch of the legislature, and has to get through the same work as the House of Commons. Man for man, its leading speakers are well worth attending to: yet they are rarely able to infuse interest into the listless atmosphere of the chamber to which they belong. They know that the people, which is intently watching every speech which is uttered in the House of Commons, hardly deigns to turn to the report of their own proceedings. Instead, therefore, of either making speeches or listening to speeches in which no one takes an interest, they dispose of their business without talk, and go home to dine. No long debates, no speeches made in the interest of mere delay, arrest the progress of legislation. If expedition be the test of efficiency, the House of Lords is the most efficient of legislatures. Yet let those who complain the loudest of the disrepute into which the House of Commons has fallen, mark the contrast. Such obstruction even as the House of Commons has to deal with is preferable to the lot which has fallen to the House of Lords.

Obstruction, then, is the clearest proof of the influence and importance of the House of Commons. Yet it does not consequently follow that obstruction is an evil which ought to be left unremedied. Free government implies government by the majority of the people, and, in any state which is self-governed, the majority in the long run must rule. Individual liberty, however, is usually prized the most in those nations which have established autonomy; and individual liberty may, of course, be sacrificed by the tyranny of a majority as effectually as it may be destroyed by the tyranny of an autocrat. Those states, therefore, which have made most progress in the work of self-government, have shown most respect for the rights of individuals, or for the rights of groups of individuals comprising minorities. It is this respect which has made obstruction possible. The House of Commons has hesitated to deprive the minority of its most important weapon. Yet it must sooner or later reflect that majorities as well as minorities have their rights, which are, to say the least, equally deserving of consideration. Self-government would be a mere delusion if the drag of the Opposition had as much force as the motive power of the Government.

As a general rule the House of Commons sits on five out of the six working days of each week. On Mondays, Tuesdays, Thursdays, and Fridays it meets at four ; on Wednesdays at noon. On Wednesdays, the business, whatever stage it may be in, is interrupted at a quarter before six ; on the other days it is continued till it is either completed, or until the House thinks proper to adjourn. Mondays, Thursdays, and Fridays are reserved for government orders ; Tuesdays for notices of motions ; Wednesdays for the orders of independent members. On Mondays and Thursdays the government is able to commence the regular business of the evening with the consideration of its ordinary business. On Fridays, Committee of Supply or Committee of Ways and Means is placed as the first order of the day. As, however, any member may intercept the motion for going into committee with some other resolution, the government business on Fridays is frequently or usually postponed till a very late hour. It may, therefore, be broadly stated that, under ordinary circumstances, government bills are dealt with on Mondays and Thursdays ; motions are discussed on Tuesdays and Fridays ; and the bills of independent members on Wednesdays ; or, when the government business is concluded, on Mondays and Thursdays ; when the debates on motions are finished on Tuesdays, and when the debates on motions and the work of committee are completed on Fridays.

Part of the time of the House, it will be thus seen, is at the disposal of the government ; part of it is at the disposal of such private members as are fortunate enough to secure precedence for their proposals. But, as government can usually command a majority of supporters, and as its own time has proved insufficient for its ordinary work, it has been of late years in the habit of trenching more and more on the time of private members. Occasionally in the case of great debates it has induced independent members to give up their own evenings, so as to allow the discussion to be continued, with little or no interruption, on the four days of the week in which the House of Commons holds evening sittings. More usually the House has allowed the government to fix supplementary, or, as they are inaccurately called, morning sittings, on Tuesdays and Fridays. When the House holds a morning sitting it meets at two in the afternoon and sits till seven o'clock in the evening, when it adjourns till nine, at which hour the independent members are allowed to commence their postponed business. The scheme, therefore, is openly designed to rob Peter to pay Paul; it deprives the independent member of a certain portion of his time, and confers it upon the government. It may be doubted whether the injury, which it thus inflicts on the independent legislator, is not much greater than the advantage which it confers on the ministry. The members, exhausted with a morning sitting, neglect to return to their duties at nine. The members of the government, having no interest in the proceedings, encourage their absence. When the House meets at nine, an insufficient number of members is in attendance, the House is counted, and as forty members are not present,[1] it is adjourned. The private members, therefore, instead of losing the five hours of the evening from four to nine, frequently lose the whole

[1] Any member of the House of Commons has a right to draw attention to the fact that forty members are not present, and to move that the House be counted. After an interval the Speaker proceeds to count the House; and if forty members are not present the House is adjourned. In the House of Lords the quorum is only of three lords.

sitting. But the government does not obtain any equivalent advantage. The House when it meets at two, meets in ill-humour. Professional men, and men of business, attend at inconvenience to themselves. Much time is frequently wasted over preliminary questions and notices, and, when the debate once commences, it is conducted under the knowledge that it must either close or be adjourned before seven. Nothing is more fatal to progress. When members opposed to a measure know that the time of the House is limited, they have a strong temptation to speak against time. Half a dozen persons, endowed with average intellect and average lungs, can easily occupy half-a-dozen hours in this way; and the government accordingly finds only too frequently that, after having sacrificed the independent members and put professional members to inconvenience, it has made no progress at all worthy of the price which has been paid for it.

The inducement to talk against time, which is encouraged by the existence of morning sittings, is frequently visible on Wednesdays. At the morning sitting the member knows that the debate must be suspended if it do not come to an end before seven o'clock. On the Wednesday sitting every member knows that the measure will be virtually lost if the debate on it is not concluded before six o'clock, or more accurately, before a quarter to six. The easiest way, therefore, of defeating a measure on a Wednesday is to talk against time; and there is more room for surprise that the expedient is not more frequently adopted, than that measures should now and then be talked out on Wednesdays. The encouragement to useless talk which is thus afforded by day sittings on Wednesdays, and by morning sittings on Tuesdays and Fridays, receives a fresh impulse on evening sittings from another rule. With much good sense the House has determined that it will not commence the consideration of any opposed order after half-past twelve at night. Suppose, for instance, on a government night, the Irish Land Bill, the Bankruptcy Bill, and the Rivers Conservancy Bill are the three first orders of the day. The debate on the Irish Land Bill is adjourned at a quarter to one. Under ordinary circumstances the debate on the Bankruptcy Bill would commence, but, if any member has placed a notice on the notice paper of his intention to oppose the Bankruptcy Bill, the half-past twelve rule operates, and the House proceeds to the consideration of the next order. The half-past twelve o'clock rule has only existed for a short period, but it has been constantly advocated for the last forty years. Parliamentary life would be almost intolerable if it were not for its existence. Every member who was bent on opposing any measure which happened to be placed among the orders of the day, would be compelled to sit up to an indeterminate hour in the morning, lest the bill which he was interested in resisting should happen to come on. But, though the rule saves the majority of members from an intolerable labour of this character, it has the concurrent disadvantage that it tends to encourage talk. A member, interested in opposing a bill, knows, if he give notice of opposition, that the bill cannot even be discussed if it is not reached before half-past twelve. Instead of waiting to fight the particular measure, it is his easiest course to take care that the preceding debate, on some other measure, shall not be stopped before the fatal hour. He makes an useless speech on Irish land to avoid making a useful speech on bankruptcy. This state of things is, perhaps, inevitable; but it is none the less true that a regulation, intended to promote the convenience of individuals, has had a tendency to increase the onflow of almost endless talk.

The ever-increasing tendency to talk which is thus encouraged by the regulations of the House of Commons is also fostered by a variety of other circumstances. The first and most obvious of these is the spread of parliamentary reporting. The easiest way in which a member can display his activity to his constituents is to speak in the House of Commons; and some members probably speak not for the purpose of producing any effect on the House, but for the sake of creating a favourable impression on the electors of the borough or of the county which they have the privilege of representing. In the old days, before the Reform Act, newspaper reports were so meagre and the circulation of the newspapers so limited, that the inducement did not exist. The patrons, moreover, who returned the mass of the members to Parliament only cared for the way in which their representatives voted or the prices which they paid for their seats, and paid no attention to their speeches. This state of things was altered by the Reform Act of 1832, and has been still further altered by the Reform Act of 1867. The modern member is usually a gentleman who has gained some reputation in his own neighbourhood; and who imagines that the success which he has achieved at home qualifies him to shine in a wider circle. Accustomed to be listened to with attention by his constituents, he naturally thinks it his first duty to speak in Westminster; and he has not acquired the art of Menelaus to speak "no more than just the thing he ought." It is not untrue, therefore, to say that the proportion of members who wish to speak is continually increasing; that the inducements to speak are becoming annually greater; and that the regulations of the House itself has added fresh inducements to do so.

Parliament, then, contains a constantly-increasing proportion of talkers; and men who, in the first instance, talk to please their constituents, go on talking for the sake of delaying measures which they dislike. It is obvious that as a long session only endures from 1,100 or 1,200 hours, and as there are 658 members of Parliament, the determination of each member to occupy, in the aggregate, only two hours of time, or to make eight speeches a quarter of an hour long each, would make all legislative progress impossible. Talk happily only arises on a few measures every session. The bulk of the bills laid before Parliament are passed almost without discussion. But the time is fast coming when the bills, whose progress is seriously contested, cannot be passed unless some limit is placed upon talk. A minority, it is obvious, can make legislation impracticable by talking against time.

A natural reluctance to interfere with the great right of talk has indeed hitherto prevented Parliament from adopting this course, and other expedients have been accordingly suggested to obviate the difficulty. A favourite plan has been the formation of grand committees, and the reference of all bills not to a committee of the whole House but to a grand committee consisting of a section of the House. One committee, it is thought, might take all bills dealing with finance, another all bills dealing with land, a third all bills dealing with education, and so on. But, in the first place, the proposal would not destroy all opportunity for talk, and in the next place, no one has been able to define any principle on which the grand committees should be composed. A system, indeed, which referred all English bills to English members, all Scotch bills to Scotch members, and all Irish bills to Irish members, would have a great deal to recommend it to some people, since it would at any rate insure that no measure should be applied to any part of the United Kingdom without the consent of its own representatives. But such a system is unlikely to commend itself to a legislature which unfortunately thinks it periodically necessary, however much it may be matter for regret, to apply coercion to Ireland.

Failing then any such remedy nothing apparently remains but to apply a limit to talk. Talk can be limited in many ways. In the first place at the present time a member is able to raise a debate on any subject by moving the adjournment of the House. This power has on some occasions proved useful; on the great majority of occasions it is simply inconvenient, the certain inconvenience outweighs the possibility of use, and the power itself should be withdrawn. The same thing may be said of the incessant motions frequently made at the end of an evening for the adjournment of the debate or the adjournment of the House. If the House decides that the debate shall not be adjourned it ought not to be open to any other member to raise immediately the same issue. The present rule, which enables member after member to challenge a division on the same question, may operate for delay. It cannot operate for efficiency.

But these changes, though they would tend to facilitate business, would still leave countless opportunities for unnecessary talk, and unnecessary talk can only be checked by a limit being placed on it. Such a limit might undoubtedly be placed in two ways. The House might say that no member should speak for more than a certain number of minutes on any subject, or that no debate should last for above a certain number of hours. But arbitrary rules of this character are open to one fatal objection. They place every subject on the same level, while every subject requires different treatment. A member may speak with much advantage for an hour on one subject, while he would be wasting time in occupying ten minutes on another. Instead, therefore, of laying down arbitrary rules for every emergency, it would be wiser and better to deal with each case on its own merits. It ought to be open for the House, as a House, to determine that a particular subject had been sufficiently debated, or that a particular member had occupied enough time.

It is, of course, true that the majority of members shrink from the exercise of arbitrary powers of this character. The great right of talk seems an indispensable part of the right of free government; and a proposal to enable a majority to stop a minority from talking seems to many persons an unjustifiable act of tyranny. Yet talk has assumed such portentous proportions that Parliament, in the last few months, has allowed this to be done. It has enabled a House of a certain size by a definite majority to declare a measure urgent. Where a measure has been declared urgent it has vested the Speaker as chairman with excessive powers; and it has even enabled the majority to say that, at a certain time, the question shall be put without further debate, or when the House is in committee that the amendments shall be put one after another without discussion. But these powers, though they were perhaps forced on the House by particular circumstances, will probably appear to future historians arbitrary measures. That, indeed, must be an arbitrary rule which is invented in a particular conjuncture to coerce a particular minority, and which is not applicable on ordinary occasions. The rule ceases to be arbitrary, which is equally applicable to all men and all parties, and which is not, therefore, directed against a particular class. It may indeed be thought that the rule loses most of its terror from the circumstance that it can only be enforced in a full House by a large majority. But the clearest thinkers will probably conclude that this condition makes it especially objectionable. Minorities, if they require protection at all, require it not when they are strong, but when they are weak. A rule which cannot be used to coerce a powerful minority, but which can be used to coerce a weak minority, protects the minority which is quite capable of taking care of itself, but does not help the minority which it is conceivable may require assistance.

Two things, therefore, seem tolerably plain. The first is that, if power be given to close a debate, or to stop a speech, it should be entrusted to a bare majority. It may be desirable to stipulate that the power should only be exercised in a House of a certain size; it cannot be desirable that the majority should be of certain proportions. The second thing is equally manifest. If new rules are to be introduced they should apply to all cases, and not be applicable to particular measures only. The best friends of the House of Commons will admit that new regulations are necessary. But what is wanted are new rules for the conduct of its ordinary business, not exceptional regulations for the conduct of its urgent measures.

Such rules have been made in previous periods.

During the first third of this century a member presenting a petition to Parliament could raise a debate upon it. The privilege originally caused little inconvenience. Petitions were only occasionally presented to Parliament. During the first five years of Pitt's administration there were not 200 petitions a year. In the five years preceding 1815 the House received an average of only 1,000 petitions a year. In the five years ending 1831 it received an average of 5,000 petitions a year. In the five years ending 1843 it received an average of nearly 20,000 petitions a year. The debating of petitions, said an high authority, threatened to become its sole business, and the House of Commons accordingly found it essential to adopt new rules to meet a new and unforeseen contingency. In 1833 it decided on holding morning sittings on two days in each week for the express purpose of receiving and discussing petitions. This rule, however, did not satisfy any one; and the House in 1835 determined, instead of holding special sittings for the debating of petitions, to discourage such debates altogether. Mere discouragement, however, did not answer its purpose. An understanding that the House did not like a debate did not prevent a member from raising one. And in 1842 it was consequently found necessary to stop the debate of all petitions. It was then decided that, except in the case of present personal grievance, or of privilege, or where immediate action was necessary, no debate on any petition should be allowed. The position of the House of Commons now is not wholly dissimilar from that in which it found itself in 1833. It is smothered by talk. Its difficulty then was removed by forbidding all debate on petitions. It can only relieve itself from its present embarrassments by taking power to stop useless and objectless discussion.

Some people, however, will probably think that the present difficulties of the House of Commons arise not merely from the length of talk, but from the conduct of a small section of its members in disregarding its orders, and in defying the authority of the Chair. The history of Parliamentary manners has not yet been written. The research which such a work would require will not probably commend it to the book-makers of the present day. But any one, if any one there be, who has mastered the contents of Hansard during the reign of George III., George IV., and William IV., will probably doubt whether Parliamentary manners have experienced the change for the worse which many persons assume, and which most persons deplore. He who will turn to the record of the quarrel between Brougham and Canning in 1823; who will recollect that in 1832 one great lawyer speaking in one House was pleased to describe another great lawyer sitting in the other House as a wasp and a bug; that the Parliamentary session of 1835 led to one duel and to four quarrels nearly resulting in duels; and that in 1840 O'Connell described the Tories as "beastly in their uproar and bellowing," and was not compelled to withdraw his words; will probably conclude that the manners of our fathers' time were not better than the manners of our own. Scenes, disgraceful to those who caused them, have from time to time occurred in the House of Commons, and their temporary cessation in previous history has been due, not to the mere improvement of manners, but to the firmness of the Speaker. He who will read the history of the Parliament which met in 1837, and which was dissolved in 1841, will be struck with the constant disorder which disgraced it under one Speaker during the first half of its existence, and with the comparative order which prevailed under another Speaker during the last half of its existence ; and will perhaps conclude that the question of order and disorder very much depends on the character of the gentleman who occupies the Chair.

If this conclusion be correct, it is manifest that the true method of preserving order is to increase the power of the Chair. Of late years the House of Commons has taken this course. The Speaker names a disorderly member to the House. The leader of the House moves his suspension during the sitting, and a member suspended three times is disqualified from sitting and voting during the rest of the session. The intention of the rule is excellent, but it may be doubted whether the penalty inflicted is desirable. If the House suspend a member from his duties, it not merely punishes the member, it simultaneously disfranchises the electors whom he represents. It ought to be possible to accomplish the one object without risking the other result. If, for instance, the member disregarding the authority of the Chair was committed to the custody of the Serjeant-at-arms till he apologised for his offence, and paid the fees consequent on his committal, the member could resume his duties almost immediately on making an adequate apology and on paying what would virtually be a fine.

These reflections, however, though they naturally emanate from the preceding narrative, have no immediate connection with the objects of this little work. It was its promise in its opening pages to trace the growth of the British Parliament, to describe its privileges, and to explain its procedure. That promise, in the intervening pages, it has been attempted to fulfil. It has been shown how the Parliament, sprung from small beginnings, was developed as the nation developed, and gradually assumed its existing shape. It has been shown how one estate of the Parliament obtained by slow degrees supremacy in the State. Like the grain of mustard-seed, which was originally less than all the seeds, it has grown into a tree which is greater than all the herbs. People of many nations and of many climes lodge under its branches. For centuries they have relied on the protection of its shadow and been sustained, when they were drooping, by its fruit. Far distant be the day when there may be no fruit on its branches, and no shadow beneath its boughs.

THE END.